CALLED

How One Couple
Served a City

CALLED

How One Couple
Served a City

by Sheridan Hill

Real Life Stories, LLC

CALLED:
HOW ONE COUPLE SERVED A CITY

by Sheridan Hill

©2014 Sheridan Hill and JoeAnn Ballard

U.S. Library of Congress Control Number: 2014907694

Real Life Stories, LLC
PO Box 248
Montreat, NC 28757
828-785-2828

www.RealLifeStories.com

Memoir / Biography

All rights reserved. No part of this publication may be reproduced, stored in a retrieval system or transmitted in any form or by any means, digital, electronic, mechanical, photocopying or otherwise, without prior permission of the publisher.

ISBN: 978-0-9791355-4-5

Editor: Dale Evva Gefland
Cover Design: Rick Soldin
Interior Design: Kathleen Beall Meyer

Table of Contents

HAVING BEEN BORN INTO A POOR COAL-mining family in the hills of West Virginia, I have personal experience with the challenges of rising above difficult circumstances. It is with this perspective that I cracked the pages of *Called* and began reading the story of JoeAnn Ballard's challenges and triumphs. Without proselytizing or preaching, she simply let the day-to-day decisions and actions of her own life stand as a quiet illustration of service.

When I began reading, I could not stop until I finished the final page. I marveled at the heart-warming stories of how she overcame many different obstacles to raise her "children." I laughed, I cried, and then I prayed that God would make me into the servant leader that Dr. Ballard so beautifully models.

JoeAnn's life shines like a jewel throughout these pages. Reading about her quiet way of serving community, we are inspired to follow Dr. Ballard's example. Day after day, year after year, she extended Christ-like compassion to the hearts and lives in need around her. She overcame family setbacks, racial prejudice, poverty, and bias against women in ministry to become a legendary leader. She is a modern-day hero who exemplifies transformational leadership at its highest level.

— Stan Toler, D.Div.
General Superintendent Emeritus
Church of the Nazarene

HAWAIIAN SUN DRIZZLED GOLD OVER THE spring of 2012 when Hank Herrod phoned me in far-flung Kauai, Hawaii. Herrod, an M.D. and Senior Fellow at the Urban Child Institute in Memphis, was on a mission to find a biographer for a relentlessly service-oriented woman in Memphis with a remarkable story. Given away by her parents when she was only a few months old, JoeAnn Ballard had raised 75 foster children— without taking a penny of federal or state money. After briefing me, Hank put JoeAnn on the phone.

"Listen," she said, "I did all this through Christ, but when people read my story, I don't want them to feel pressured into serving Christ or serving their fellow man. Because the minute you do that, you've enslaved the person."

I felt an immediate resonance with her words. The opportunity to write JoeAnn's book was a glorious reason to leave the paradise of Kauai, where I was temporarily living, and return to Black Mountain, North Carolina.

It has been a great honor to work with JoeAnn, her daughter Ephie, Hank Herrod, Gene Cashman, and so many smart, bright-hearted people who serve the South's materially poor. JoeAnn graciously provided materials dating back several decades, including those that would allow me to bring to life her husband, the "mountain of a man," who died in 2008. I read Monroe's homespun autobiography, perused his pocket-sized notebooks of neatly written "to-do" lists with names, needs, and measurements. I interviewed those who had known and loved him and watched the videos of his funeral service.

Delving into JoeAnn and Monroe Ballard's journey, following the trail to the phenomenal work of the Neighborhood Christian Center, has lifted my heart time and time again. Their belief that, despite the odds, all would work out buoys my own faith. At a universal level, their conviction that when helping someone you must take care not to enslave them opens up a critical perspective.

Most curious is the question posed to us all through the Ballards' lives. It is the query ruthlessly held up by Henri Nouwen, Donald McNeill, and Douglas Morrison in their book *Compassion*: "Are we really servants when we can say when, where, and how long we will give of our time and energy?" Maybe I can't be utterly selfless like the Ballards, but I can bravely keep asking the question: How do I serve?

— Sheridan Hill

THE STORY OF JOEANN AND MONROE BALLARD
is a tale of radical servanthood born in the South of the
1950s. Their work is a powerful model for us all, a living example
of what happens when two people come together, create a vision of
serving their neighbors, and refuse to let go of it—no matter what
happens. By following their hearts, they modeled compassion at
the everyday, true-grit level.

The Ballards were a different breed of Baby Boomer. Rather
than accumulating wealth for themselves, they saw the needs of
their neighbors and refused to turn a blind eye. Eventually they
raised seventy-five children—without so much as a penny of state
or federal money. Through the years, their compassionate acts
birthed a thriving nonprofit organization that continues to touch
the lives of thousands of neighbors in need each year: the Neighborhood Christian Center in Memphis, Tennessee.

This was no small feat for a city that is half white and half
black, a city where slaves were bought and sold to service the cotton market and the city where civil rights leader Rev. Dr. Martin
Luther King Jr. was shot down in cold blood.

Living on meager incomes, JoeAnn and Monroe never dwelled
on the things they didn't have. Their thoughts were always on others. "We felt that our investment in someone else was the most
important thing we could do with our lives," JoeAnn says, "and it
felt good to see young people thriving and making something out
of themselves."

With unwavering focus, the Ballards strove to model what
might be possible if people of means worked—in the right way—

with people who have nothing. They set their sights on what Joe-Ann calls "a Christ-centered way of serving those in need." It is not a stretch to say that the bridges erected by the Ballards more than three decades ago gave the white community greater access to the needs of their brethren in North Memphis. More importantly, they gave the affluent a reason to care.

"They brought people into their vision," says Larry Jensen, a longtime leader in the Memphis business community and ardent supporter of the Neighborhood Christian Center. "Because of the Ballards, I realized two things. One, I didn't know anything about my neighbors who weren't like me. Two, I didn't care."

How did a materially poor Memphis couple create such bounty for so many people for so long?

You could say it was the force of their personalities or because they are generous people. Lots of Christians will argue the Ballards succeeded because of their fierce obeisance to Christian values, that they couldn't have done it without their faith.

Jenson explains, "JoeAnn and Monroe got these people off the side of the road, cleaned them up, bandaged their wounds, and said, 'Now we're going in a different direction. Then they held them accountable to take advantage of what God gave them to improve their own lives."

For JoeAnn, faith is a day-by-day, moment-by-moment trust. "I never wavered from a simple trust in God," she says. "It's not complex. It's just, 'Lord I don't know what to do. Help me.' Somehow, I was chosen by God to do this work, and I took it seriously. I figured out early on that I couldn't just talk to people about Christ," she says. "I had to be the hands and feet of Christ."

Wherever they went, JoeAnn and Monroe turned strangers into family. Monroe's fatherly compassion for students at Douglass Elementary eventually became the hearthstone of the Neighborhood Christian Center in Memphis. Seeing a need in the disadvantaged children of others, the Ballards took them home and loved them as if they were their own.

JoeAnn refers to the people she helped as her "children" even though most of them were teenagers and young adults. It's not really accurate to call them foster children since none of the relationships were initiated, formalized, or funded through any federal or county departments; yet for lack of a better term they have always been called the Ballard foster children.

Rather than work through an institution, the Ballards responded from their hearts and thereby avoided the worst errors of federal programs and Christian compassionate ministries. As JoeAnn puts it, "We simply try to change a person's heart by showing that we care."

Ultimately this mission brought hope to hundreds of people who drank from the Ballards' font of compassion until they could stand on their own two feet. Until they were so full, they had to give back. One by one, as many of them reached the tipping point from grateful receiver to willing giver, JoeAnn refused to let them try to pay her back. Neither did she advise them to "pass it on" as is common in the ministry and other social models. "The minute you tell a person to pass it on, you've just enslaved them," she says. "I wanted our children to know that everything we gave them, we gave through love. No strings. We tried to serve as models for giving." As the descendant of slaves, her words are singularly profound.

Nowadays there is plenty of giving in Memphis. It is the second-most-generous major city in the nation, according to a per capita giving report in the August 2012 *Chronicle of Philanthropy*. But money alone cannot solve the grinding problems of the poor.

Today, after billions of dollars in failed federal and state poverty programs and quick fixes have swirled down the drain, experts realize that these efforts have only served to deepen the social and emotional demarcation line between the haves and the have-nots. Close observers now conclude what JoeAnn and Monroe Ballard knew long ago: poverty is the result of broken relationships, so the only way to impact poverty is relationally.

While emergency aid is often necessary, the ultimate goal is not to give money, food, and material goods but to build relationships. There is little point in giving a family a Christmas dinner each December if they are not regularly engaged at the personal level. Steve Corbett and Brian Fikkert concluded that the goal is "to walk with the materially poor so they are better stewards of their lives and communities, including their material needs." (*When Helping Hurts*, 2012, p. 113).

JoeAnn and Monroe had ample room in their huge hearts for those in need. Because they opened their hearts, they opened their home. Although they had precious little, living off the salary of a public schoolteacher working with low-income children, their marriage became a living example of loaves and fishes: the more they shared, the more they had. Their friend and supporter Gene Cashman sees their miraculous work through the Christian perspective. "It's a matter of how you use your talents—and as you use your talents, they are multiplied. You are given more to do more with."

IT IS SIX O'CLOCK ON A FRIDAY EVENING IN JULY. JoeAnn Ballard is sunk deep in an armchair with her ever-present laptop in place. A sense of satisfaction lingers like an aura around her. She is working just outside her former office at the Neighborhood Christian Center.

The room labeled "CEO" now belongs to her eldest daughter, Ephie—JoeAnn relinquished the day-to-day grind of the center in 2008, when her title was changed to senior adviser.

But JoeAnn cannot stop serving.

Serving is not what she does; it is who she is.

Her eyes are always roaming the room for the person who needs help. She can't get excited by prospects of retiring and going to Europe or vacationing in Hawaii. If JoeAnn goes out of town, she wants to know where the poor people live. She wants to find the people who need help.

JoeAnn, a handful of staffers, and several volunteers are working at a steady pace to prepare for Lovebuilders, a couples empowerment program offered by the Neighborhood Christian Center. Tonight's meal (cooked from scratch onsite), childcare, inspirational speakers, and financial-responsibility workshop are free to participating couples. That's how the center works: everything is accomplished intimately, with care, and in the spirit of joy in serving.

Today the stately and enthusiastic "Miss Ephie"—Ephie Jean Ballard Johnson—has spent much of the afternoon making repeated phone calls on behalf of a client we'll call Mary. Mary is running out of time and straddling the mortgage-qualifying hurdles set up by the Veteran's Administration. With the help of NCC staff, Mary's loan is approved at 4:30, just before the weekend starts.

Down the hall, in the center's shiny commercial kitchen, volunteers and staffers slice juicy ribs from racks, spill cookies onto paper plates, and put out enough napkins, plastic ware, and soft drinks for thirty-five couples. The succulent aroma of slow-cooked barbeque fills the air. Ephie's husband, Rodney Johnson, and one of the Lovebuilders participants, Stanley Tate, have spent the afternoon patiently toiling over a large smoker made out of an oil drum. With the devotion of master chefs, they repeatedly slathered homemade sauce over 140 pounds of pork ribs and 40 pounds of chicken wings.

"Taste this," says NCC employee Herman Britton, holding out a sample of the gleaming meat. "All of this was donated by a local rancher," Herman says, waving a butcher knife over sauce-glazed fresh-pork ribs and chicken wings.

Herman is, you might say, an NCC devotee.

Twenty years ago when he was looking for work, JoeAnn and Monroe Ballard gave him a home at the original NCC facility and sent him for a job interview nearby at the Cozy Corner barbeque place. Monroe took Herman under his wing, offering love and fatherly attention. Herman worked his way up the ranks at the Neighborhood Christian Center and today works full time as the Department of Operations manager.

"I've worked hard all my life," he says. "I came from farm work, seasonal jobs. Living at the Neighborhood Christian Center for two and a half years, I was able to save my money. Now, because of the Ballards, I own my own home." Herman looks across the kitchen at his wife, Ester—who was also taken in by the Ballards as a young woman—and smiles. "Mr. and Mrs. Ballard changed my life."

~ ONE ~
A Mississippi Childhood

AS JOEANN MARSHALL STOOD ON THE STEPS of the Nazarene Bible Institute, a warm breeze brushed her face. She trembled a little, despite the mild May weather. Three years of Bible college were ending, and she had nowhere to go. All the sacrifice she had made, right down to shredding her fingers picking the last gleanings of cotton in her uncle's field in the summers—what was it all for?

JoeAnn had given up secular education at Prentiss Institute for Bible college because she felt a calling. Sometimes the quest for God rose up in her like a tidal wave—but how to respond to it wasn't exactly clear. Often she thought of a teenaged Florence Nightingale, whose heart too had been pierced with a call to compassion. In thousands of pages of writings she left behind, Nightingale describes a painful awareness of the suffering of others, particularly European soldiers fighting in the Crimean War.

Thwarting her family's wishes, she traveled to the wounded soldiers, set up nursing stations, and trained other women to help. Kneeling in the dirt, Nightingale bound their wounds, assisted in amputations, and nursed them through cholera and typhus outbreaks. Against the medical conventions of the day, she stressed better diet as well as washing the soldiers and keeping their linens as clean as possible as a way of both decreasing the mortality rate and helping to heal their malnourished hearts.

Along with her medical ministrations, Nightingale wrote letters for soldiers unable to do so themselves and wrote to their families when they died. She set up reading rooms with books and coffee for soldiers at a time when only bars and lounges were available to them. In personal essays, Nightingale dared to wonder if the world could imagine a woman who resembles Christ.

Nightingale's work to reduce the mortality rate of soldiers and veterans of the Crimean War was privately funded over the decades, allowing her to operate outside the constraints of the establishment. The idea of private funding to help the helpless made a permanent imprint on young JoeAnn's mind, nurtured by her foster father, who read the Nightingale biography to her at bedtime.

JoeAnn was clear about two things: she wanted to serve God, and she wanted to serve the poor and needy. But no churches in 1965 were clamoring for a young, inexperienced minister who happened to be female and black. Exasperated, she wondered what a farm girl from Lucedale, Mississippi, was doing in a West Virginia Bible college, anyway. And why, as some of her older relatives liked to inquire, didn't she have a husband yet? But amidst the uncertainty of what lay before her, the young woman had— she searched for the word to describe it—a *knowing*. While part of her was clamoring and complaining that things should be different, another part of her had the feeling that somehow it was all going to work out.

Young as she was, JoeAnn wanted to help others the way her foster parents had supported her and her brother and sister, lifting them like flowers toward the sun. JoeAnn's foster parents, who were distant blood relatives, had set the bar for selflessness, generosity, and thrift. Never had JoeAnn heard them offer the tiniest resentment toward her biological mother and father, who—truth be told—had abandoned their children.

As the family story goes, a few days before Christmas 1944, JoeAnn's father, Dyke Sylvester Marshall, packed the three kids in his Chevy sedan, drove them away from their home at 1750 Virginia Street in Mobile, and never brought them back.

Their mother, Lacy Lee Lawrence, was a girl of nineteen; Dyke was twenty-six. As Dyke drove away from the Gulf Coast into rural Mississippi, JoeAnn's birth certificate was in the glove box. It listed Dyke's occupation as shipyard worker and was signed by a midwife rather than a licensed physician. Like most black babies at that time, JoeAnn had been delivered at home by a midwife. There weren't any black doctors, and white doctors rarely ventured into the black part of town.

Dyke drove into the basin lands, shadowing the Pascagoula River where pine trees were scarred from long cuts made to siphon off the turpentine. Where scuppernong and other wild grape vines stood bare, waited for spring's warmth to return. Where picked-over cotton fields stood with their bronze-colored stalks and the occasional white-puff face, watching the cars pass.

Dyke was headed with his babies to Lucedale, the county seat of George County, and Lacy Lee's grandfather's place. Down Rural Route 3 was a rectangle of rural forest and swampland anchoring southern Mississippi. Here, families stuck together in southern custom—but in reality it was the only way to survive, especially for black people. When the residents of Lucedale saw the big fancy car speeding through the town's one stoplight, they speculated about who it was because everybody knew everybody else—and most of them were related somewhere down the line. If a stranger showed up in town and got to talking with an old-timer from Lucedale, before long she'd have figured out how you were related.

At the end of a muddy, bumpy road, Dyke pulled up to the old farmhouse where DeLoach and Ora Mae Benjamin lived. He lifted three-month old JoeAnn from a blanket on the floor of the car, then looked at his other two children. The oldest, Lula, was three; the middle child, Dyke, Jr., could barely walk. "Come on now," he called, taking Dyke, Jr.'s arm and pulling him out of the car with his free hand.

DeLoach, like most of the men in his family, had served in the U.S. military in a time when many African Americans were just one or two generations away from the gruesome days of slavery. DeLoach was the father of two children with his first wife, who had died young, leaving him to raise their two teenagers on his own. But his single-parenting days had just begun.

When DeLoach's sister died, she left eighteen children behind, and he took in every single one of them. By the time he married Ora Mae Tanner, DeLoach was in his early fifties. He hadn't had much time to himself, but he didn't feel the need for it. He preferred to live surrounded by family, working with a bright heart and two strong hands to make a good life out of what little they had. As for Ora Mae, her parents were dead, and she was living alone on the Lawrence farm.

Originally the Lawrence family—JoeAnn's ancestors—owned as many as eight hundred acres distributed among twelve siblings. In the extended Lawrence family, one relative, Quitman Wells, owned fifteen hundred acres. According to JoeAnn's relative Charles L. Grant Sr. in his book *Heritages from Our Foundation Fathers,* in the early 1800s the requirements for acquiring a homestead of up to 160 acres were simple: File an application, spend every night on the property for two years, and get the neighbors to attest to this fact. The homesteader was then issued a patent deed stating that the parcel would belong to him and his heirs forever.

Ora Mae's father, Sardin Tanner, was mulatto, which almost always meant the offspring of a white slave owner and a black female slave. Her mother was Georgianna Lawrence, whose parents were Dan and Elizabeth Brown Lawrence. When Sardin married Georgianna, she was a teenager living with her parents and raising her little boy, Lacey Lawrence. Aside from being landowners, the Lawrences of Alabama were well-known as leaders in the community and included preachers, Sunday-school teachers, educators at historically black universities, and owners of such establishments as a café, a beauty shop, a barber shop, a funeral home, and washeterias.

DeLoach's marriage to Ora Mae Tanner was fruitful in love— but not in progeny. He was pondering that very thing when he heard Dyke Marshall's shiny, late-model car pull into the yard, alarming the chickens. The old front door of the hand-hewn farmhouse creaked as DeLoach opened it. He was mildly surprised to see a little family heading for him, only slowly recognizing the man who had married Lacy Lee, his wife's niece, who was ten years younger than Dyke. *So, these are the little babies that have lived with all that trouble,* he thought to himself. The stories of Dyke and Lace Lee Lawrence's fighting had rippled through the family for years.

"Can you help us out?" Dyke asked, holding the baby outstretched from his new suit. The children's clothes were dingy and torn. "Just for a little while," he said, breaking into a grin when DeLoach reached out for baby JoeAnn. "Till we can get back on our feet."

Childless Ora Mae appeared at the door and in a single gesture drew that baby to her bosom. After all these years of wondering why God hadn't seen fit to give her a child, she knew exactly what this moment meant. She knew that taking these kids that day might mean keeping them forever. She knew she would be cutting cotton flour sacks to hand stitch into clothes, that in addition to farm chores, she would be making many trips to the yard and back, hauling well water inside for drinking, cooking, and cleaning. And she knew she would have taken these children in even if they hadn't shared the same blood. As the two older children looked up from the doorway, the chilly winter air suddenly seemed to warm, and DeLoach and Ora Mae embraced their first foster children, welcoming them into their hearts and hearth.

JoeAnn saw her mother only a few times after that day. The kids didn't know that Lacy Lee had called Ora Mae a few weeks after Dyke had dropped them off, explaining that they were getting divorced and asking Ora Mae if she would raise the kids for her. Dyke came around once or twice a year, always on a holiday when there was sure to be plenty of food. Each year at Mardi Gras time, Ora Mae took JoeAnn, Dyke Jr., and Lula back to Mobile to see their father. But if he ever sent one dime of support for the children, JoeAnn never heard of it. It wasn't long before the older children stopped asking—or caring—if their parents were coming back to get them. It hardly mattered as God had blessed DeLoach and Ora Mae with enough love, thrift, and stubborn determination to parent many children who were not their own. Over time, they wound up taking in an additional twenty-five children from the Basin community, about twelve miles from Lucedale, Mississippi. They could not overlook the sight of a child whose parents hadn't the means, or perhaps the courage, to care for their babies. Over and over again, they allowed others' burdens to become their blessings. It was a way of life that imprinted permanently on Joe-Ann's heart. With her "real" parents absent and distant relatives acting as her real parents, the question of who to love simply dissolved: she was to love everyone.

The farm where DeLoach and Ora Mae fed all those hungry mouths had been passed down to Ora Mae from her maternal grandfather, Dan Lawrence. It was rare for a black man to own land in the South, due to laws and general conditions before the Civil War. In the 1800s white landowners had grown rich off the worldwide cotton market, picked by Mississippi's slaves—as many as a half million. Some southern states (South Carolina, Georgia, and Mississippi) had made it a crime to teach a person of color how to read or write. But by the beginning of the Civil War in 1861, a few southern whites were not only educating their slaves but also freeing them.

As Ora Mae's family told the story, their ancestor Dan Lawrence had been a slave in East Tennessee, where farms were small and the mountainous land and colder climate created fewer opportunities for cotton plantations. Freed from bondage, he gathered his wife and children and left East Tennessee for Mississippi. It is unknown how they traveled that far; perhaps he loaded them into a horse- or mule-drawn farm wagon. They wouldn't have been welcome on a white passenger train, and most of the tracks had been torn up in the war, anyway. The South was in shambles.

Arriving in Mississippi, Dan was prepared for the difficult task of building a new life. He was a fearless, big-boned man never known to shy away from physically brutal farm jobs. He could take down towering oaks with an ax, run a sawmill, and build wagons and houses. He could wrangle a cow and ride a horse and provide them with both blacksmith and veterinary services. He also became a preacher, carrying the message of the Gospel to local folks on Sundays and whenever he had a chance to spread the Good Word.

As Charles L. Grant wrote, "After these early settlers had become very well established in their homes, it was not uncommon for a man to drive to his neighbor's house some ten or more miles away and spend the day talking about the church and how God had blessed them by bringing them from under the bondage of slavery."

Dan Lawrence homesteaded on eighty acres near Lucedale, plowed with a mule and planted by hand. He understood how the phases of the moon affect the start of a crop. He found time to be a spiritual leader and cofounder of the United Methodist church in the Basin community and always had time to help one of his children and grandchildren.

It is no wonder that Dan's granddaughter Ora Mae married a man just like him. DeLoach was a big, hardworking, generous man from Little River, Alabama. He was something of an herbalist and a good cook. During World War I, he tirelessly made meals for thousands of National Guardsmen arriving at Camp McClellan, Alabama, for Army training. In the fall of 1917, there were 27,000 troops at Camp McClellan, including the First Separate Negro Company of Maryland. DeLoach was discharged in March 1919 from Company B 437, Army Reserve Labor Battalion. None of his living relatives are sure why, but one of his legs was virtually useless afterward. He was discharged with a full disability pension and used a wooden cane for the rest of his life. It became his way of emphasizing a point, often punching it into the ground and cheering a struggling child, "Never give up!"

When the spirit moved him, DeLoach would steady himself, reach down, and swoop JoeAnn onto his shoulders, saying, "Come on, Fannie"—his special nickname for her—and carry her around the farm as he tended to his tasks. DeLoach considered himself a progressive man and subscribed to *Progressive Farmer* magazine. (The all-white staff were also *socially* progressive and went so far as to print an editorial in 1960 supporting voting rights for black people.)

You might think a man with a twelve-acre farm and a bad leg would be unable to care for over forty children, but DeLoach had more love in his little finger than most people had in their whole bodies. JoeAnn called him "Montee" or "Daddy" and Ora Mae "Mama," and a slew of other people were "aunt," "uncle" and "cousin." The South was that kind of place. Everybody knew everybody else's business, like it or not. So you might as well like it. Besides, it came in handy when trouble came to town. When there was illness, neighbors would come with a cure or bring the doctor. When a member of the Basin community died, if the family didn't have the money to bury the poor soul, neighbors pitched in to donate wood, build the coffin, dig the hole, cut flowers, pay the preacher—whatever it took to give their brethren a decent burial.

Little JoeAnn liked sitting on the front porch, taking in the sweet aroma of gardenias and magnolias planted near the house. In warm weather Ora Mae's flower garden was a living canvas of roses, Easter lilies, and medicinal herbs, and nearby peach and plum trees offered their succulent fruit. In late summer etched mahogany ovals began falling from the pecan trees, and pies were sure to follow.

JoeAnn also trained her ears to decipher the sound of different engines before a car or truck came past the big old oak tree that blocked part of the view. Before she could read, she memorized the colors of different license plates and could identify a car and where it was from in a heartbeat. Often she knew whose it was. Her daddy's car never came again.

Sometimes JoeAnn looked at the Sears catalog, turning page after page of slim white women dressed in all the newest fashions. There wasn't a single black face in any of those pages or any of the other clothes catalogs. Then she realized that her baby doll and all of her friends' baby dolls were white. Black dolls were extremely rare in the United States because there was no market for them. A psychologist's study at the time showed that given the choice between a black doll and a white doll, both white and black children would choose a white one. But one year JoeAnn asked Santa for a doll with the same color skin as hers. Santa must have had to go all the way to New York City, but he found her a black baby, and it sat waiting for her on Christmas morning.

The spirit of the Christmas season penetrated the house like the fragrance from the fresh evergreen tree, chopped down from the woods by DeLoach. It was loaded with ornaments that Ora Mae embroidered and sewed by hand, and folks came from miles around each December to admire. The biggest draw, however, was Ora Mae's seasonal baking: Christmas pies of apple and pumpkin, pound cakes and chocolate cakes, and cookies made with local honey and molasses.

To everything there is a season and a purpose unto heaven. This JoeAnn understood in the marrow of her bones. Spring was for planting, summer for hoeing, fall for harvesting. Anything they didn't grow in the fields DeLoach simply hunted or harvested from the forests and fields. He knew which plants were medicinal and which were deadly and that a spider web made a fine bandage for a deep cut. Like the four seasons, the events of JoeAnn's childhood wove together in a four-part helix, forming a worldview of love, generosity, hard work, and faith.

New Year's Day was hog-killing time. A three- or four-hundred pound hog could easily feed a small family all year long, so it took two of them to see the Lawrence family through till the next winter. Butchering an animal that size required cold weather to discourage contamination. A handful of male relatives and neighbors came to help for however many days it took, and they were properly thanked with plenty of fatback and chitlins to take home for their own families. The pig parts that plantation owners historically left for slaves had quickly become a well-loved traditional meal for African Americans in the South, where story-telling was as much a part of mealtime as the food.

The meat was salt cured for a month, then sugar cured and smoked in hickory for half the spring. The resulting meat was fit for a king, and Ora Mae pressure canned it in Mason jars for safekeeping and eating the rest of the year. All the fresh fruit and garden vegetables too were peeled and cooked and canned in glass Mason jars: purple-hulled peas, Great Northern beans, turnips and collard greens, peaches, and every kind of fruit jam and jelly.

Montee and Ora Mae shouldered the exhausting chores necessary to run the farm. He fed the cows and hogs at the crack of dawn while Ora Mae milked the cows every day or sometimes twice a day. They refused to make farmhands out of their children and instead assigned them smaller but important tasks. They picked cucumbers, peas, and butter beans out of the garden for dinner. They happily ventured into the nearby woods to pick blackberries, dewberries, and huckleberries, eating their fill and sucking on the ambrosia of honeysuckle vines. The kids kept their rooms neat and took turns washing dishes and sweeping chicken litter from the dirt yard. They pumped water for the cows and carried it to their trough twice a day. JoeAnn didn't mind hauling water from the pump to the house. As she watched the cool water pour into the wooden bucket, she often thought of the man she called Daddy and how he always made things better—including the well he had dug so they wouldn't have to walk all the way to the stream to bring water to the house.

In the spacious kitchen, Ora Mae always had a fire crackling in the wood cook stove, and she'd be cooking up something good.

The cook stove was also a main source of heat for the house, besides the two fireplaces. The children slept in warmth in full-length handmade nightgowns underneath piles of cotton quilts that Ora Mae had pieced together from scraps. When they were small, Ora Mae heated large towels by the stove at bedtime, rolled them up, and pressed them under the covers of each child's bed. When they were older, the kids would come and get their own warmed towel.

In the mornings the kitchen was warm and fragrant with the smell of Louisiana coffee with chicory, biscuits, and salt-cured ham. JoeAnn would slip from under the covers, dash to the outhouse, then fly to the kitchen for a warm breakfast. She had become as strong as any boy her age and liked to run and jump and climb trees—which may have been why a neighbor boy sometimes teased her for being a tomboy. Sitting at the pine-plank table, she watched Ora Mae hover over two cast-iron frying pans, one sizzling with bacon and the other full of pancakes. "We'll have company for dinner tonight, baby," Ora Mae called over her shoulder to JoeAnn. "You can help me pluck the chickens after your brother kills them."

JoeAnn liked it when folks came into the warmth and safety of their home. It was the kind of home that people knew would provide them with help. A place where a lost soul could eat, sit on the porch, get their questions answered, stay a few nights, borrow money. A safe house. Like the early church in the book of Acts, JoeAnn learned from an early age how to share all things in common with whomever God would bring her way.

TWO
Coming of Age

IN THE 1960 CENSUS, AFRICAN AMERICANS MADE up nearly half of Mississippians but only 3 percent of the state's registered voters. Confederate flags flew from municipal buildings along with the Mississippi state flag. Racial segregation was state mandated. The result was that black folk were usually guaranteed inferior buildings and fewer resources and were completely blocked from better facilities reserved for white people. Public restrooms, drinking fountains, restaurants, public gathering places, and public transportation all specified separate areas for blacks and whites.

Segregated education generally meant all-black schools in impoverished areas of town with older versions of textbooks—and fewer of them—and primitive physical plants. There were fewer teachers too, with a student-to-teacher ratio of about 40:1. Until the 1960s it was common for a black teacher to walk several miles to work each day.

At Basin Elementary, JoeAnn did not have a textbook for the first two years of school. She looked over the shoulder of another child to follow along in class and did her best to comprehend. Some of the teachers were graduates of Tuskegee, Rust, or Florida A&M, and they accepted lower pay than their white counterparts. But black people had learned to take what was given to them and try to prosper, regardless.

By the time she was a ninth grader at Oak Grove High in Lucedale, JoeAnn was already five feet nine inches and at eye level with many of the boys, even if she was slender. As such, she suffered bullying from kids who regarded her and her siblings as foreigners in the Basin community. Moreover, since they did not live with their biological parents, other black children teased them for being misfits.

"Why is your last name different from your parents' last name?" they were sometimes asked. "Are you a bastard?" On the school bus, one boy made it his personal mission to attack JoeAnn on a regular basis. He would lord over her as she sat in her seat, pull her plaited hair, and shove her so hard that she lurched against the person sitting beside her. But he underestimated the spunk and self-respect of this black child. One day JoeAnn's frustration welled up inside of her so hard that she had to fight back. She didn't want to hurt the boy, and she did not want to get into trouble, but she needed to stop him. So she stood up and shoved him back.

The next day the headmaster called JoeAnn to his office—and gave her the beating of her life. Up and down her back and legs he went, sometimes with his hand and sometimes with a wooden paddle. While he worked on her, the yellow school bus pulled away. She had missed the bus home. For the rest of her life Joe-Ann would remember that beating and the long, shameful walk home, twelve miles in black patent leather shoes in the damp October air. With every step, she prayed for numbness to set in. It was nearly dark when she forced her legs to carry her up the dirt road to their home. When Ora Mae—who had been anxiously watching the road after JoeAnn didn't get off the bus—spotted her, JoeAnn tried not to let her face register the pain.

Ora Mae gasped. "What's wrong with you, child?"

"Momma . . ." She couldn't find words and crumpled onto the porch.

Hoping against hope that what she feared was not true, Ora Mae unbuttoned the row of white pearl buttons on the back of JoeAnn's dress. It was one of many garments Ora Mae had made by hand: a deep lavender dress embroidered with small white daisies. And there, underneath the dress were bulging bruises and bloody marks across the girl's backside. "Baby, lie down here on the sofa," she whispered. Gently pressing a cool, wet cloth on the purple welts, Ora Mae felt her own tears rise where her daughter's wouldn't. She stroked JoeAnn's forehead until the sun was low in the sky.

The next day Ora Mae arranged for her cousin to drive her to school to talk to the headmaster. She forced herself to recite the words Booker T. Washington famously wrote: "I shall allow no man to belittle my soul by making me hate him." It was a tall order. Wisely, Ora Mae did not take issue with the principal's punishment; instead, she simply built a case to move JoeAnn to another school.

"There is no way these kids are going to leave my child be," she said. "Please: let her go to Magnolia High in Moss Point." Although the town of Moss Point, Mississippi, was forty miles south, the principal agreed, and Ora Mae reasoned that her cousin could take JoeAnn to school on her way to work near Moss Point. But making the switch posed the problem of earning extra money each month to contribute to her cousin's gas bill and help with wear-and-tear on the car. People like Ora Mae and DeLoach rarely ask for favors, but if they do, they will move mountains to relieve any burden that their need might create for someone else.

To Ora Mae's already busy list of daily household and farm chores she added cleaning a white lady's house, selling more eggs, and mending and sewing more clothes for folks. For three years without complaint, Ora Mae rose before dawn and stayed up later at night to get everything done.

Magnolia High School broadened JoeAnn's small-town horizons. The teachers seemed worldly, more sophisticated, and they loaded the students into activity buses and took them on field trips out of town. Even the ride to and from school with her relatives seemed exotic as JoeAnn listened to their stories and smelled the sweet, damp smell of the nearby Gulf of Mexico.

Sometimes at bedtime, DeLoach read from Booker T. Washington's autobiography, *Up from Slavery*. Born into slavery in Virginia (his mother refused to name his white father), Washington became a great orator, cofounder of thousands of schools for black people, and a highly influential person, a master at creating networks with wealthy whites. Reading Washington's book to Joe-Ann and her siblings, DeLoach made sure the main themes were driven home: "Remember to never let your grievances overshadow your opportunities. And if you want to lift yourself up, lift up someone else."

JoeAnn was ever-mindful of the sacrifices DeLoach and Ora Mae willingly made, and she set her sights to be like them. Out of the goodness in their souls, they had taken in JoeAnn, Dyke Jr., and Lula, refusing to use the children for farmhands. What precious little they had was given completely to the children, never holding back. They gave their all and expected nothing in return.

When October came and brought the first spell of cool air, Ora Mae would say, "Feels like camp-meeting weather." And DeLoach would smile. "That's right, Mama." But she knew even before the turn of the weather because she had orders for new clothes to make. Dressing up wasn't the most important part of camp meeting, but "puttin' on the dog" (looking good) was part of paying respect to God and a way to honor the special prayer time taken out of regular routines. People would begin dropping by in late summer to ask Ora Mae to create their new camp-meeting clothes and put in their orders for homemade cakes. She would make twenty-five or thirty cakes for camp meeting.

Camp meetings had brought Protestants together in the South for a hundred years. They were usually held in the fall—when cool weather came, someone was likely to say, "Camp meetin' weather!" One of the original African American camp-meeting songs, from 1867, later became popular in white secular and nonsecular communities: "As I went down in the river to pray, studying about that good ol' way . . ." A good camp meeting might draw several thousand Protestants to what became a powerful time of prayer and conversion.

It is impossible to overstate the importance of the church in the black community. As Charles Grant wrote in his family history book, "It was common for our forefathers to worship all day and until late in the night on Sundays." At church black people felt welcome to sing their songs, pray their prayers, and testify at leisure without anyone interfering.

Historically churches took up the slack left by state governments that either forbade black education outright or neglected to provide for it in their education laws. Sunday school included teachings from the Bible as well as the blue-backed *Webster Speller*, and children were expected to learn something about science and math as well. Churches and camp meetings were a necessary hatching ground for evolution of souls and minds.

JoeAnn had grown up in the Mt. Pleasant United Methodist Church on Willie Kennedy Road in Basin, Mississippi. Although it doesn't show up on many maps, Basin is an unincorporated town about twelve miles outside of Lucedale. Here, a dozen or so black families worshipped together. The Mt. Pleasant Camp Meeting had started in the mid-1800s with white families, many of them slave owners. But in 1858 they began allowing slaves access to their religious services. Near where horses were kept, the white Methodists set out logs for their slaves to sit and listen to preaching. After the Emancipation Proclamation, the newly freed slaves wanted a campground of their own, and in 1880 JoeAnn's ancestor W. H. (Hampton) Lawrence reportedly bought ten acres for under two dollars. Praying, socializing, teaching, and preaching still continue at the Mt. Pleasant Camp Meeting.

If there was preaching going on, the Lawrences were out in full force. Aunt Emaline Lawrence was given to moving about on her knees while praying. Like Jesus, A. C. Lacey was a preacher and a carpenter who stayed busy raising homes and hearts. But the local community held high standards for their spiritual leaders, and the pulpit was revered as sacred ground. If a traveling minister came by and wanted to preach, he had to present his license before he entered the pulpit. Laypeople who wanted to address the congregants were asked to preach from the floor in front of the pulpit.

Camp meetings in particular were an outlet for pent-up emotions. When camp-meeting time came around, children were let out of school at noon that week so they could go home, do their chores, get some food, and get to meeting on time. Carless, Joe-Ann and her family walked more than an hour on the dusty road to get there. DeLoach always made sure he had good batteries in his flashlight to lead the way down the pitch-black dirt road when they walked home at night. Those who traveled far from home slept in tents at the meeting ground.

There was a weeklong slate of high-spirited preachers on fire with "the Word of God." In long black cassocks set off by a long white stole or a red one or both, a preacher stood and gave the crowd what it had come for. In undulating tones, the Word of God poured through him, and whenever he gulped for a breath, voices rose around him, sounding into the pause, giving all glory to God. Preaching started in the dark before sunup, filling the air all day long and into the night until the preacher was hoarse and the most stouthearted sinner had come to Jesus. More than once a preacher was laid out helpless on the altar from the power of the grace streaming through.

Usually several vocal congregants would gather to one side, forming the Amen Corner. It would go something like this:

> God's grace is sufficient. [Amen!] We got to find out where this load of worry comes from. [Yeah!] If His eye is on the sparrow, he is watching over me. God's not through with me. He's still working on me. That's why I'm here. [All right! All right!] Paul said the Lord will make a way out of no way. [Yes, Lord!] Brothers and sisters, you don't have to worry about a thing, just trust Him. Anyone can worry; it takes a dedicated person to pray instead of worry. We got to live our lives and do our best and leave the rest to Him. [Amen, Lord!] You got to depend on God. You got to know He makes the

27

sun shine, He makes the rain come, He always finds time to care for you. He says to place all your cares upon him. He's our Father, He cares about us, Amen. [Amen! Thank you Lord!] Think about it. He wants you to call on Him. [That's right!] If there's trouble in your home, call Him. If you don't know where to turn, call on Him. Ask and it shall be given, seek and you will find, knock and He will open the door.

As the temperature rose in the tent, the preacher wiped his face with a clean white handkerchief, stepped from the pulpit and into the narrow aisle among the people perched in folding chairs.

Prayer changes things, brothers and sisters. [Amen!] I say prayer changes things. [Yes, Lord, thank you, Lord.] How do I know? Not because anybody told me. I'm talking about something I know. I've been through all kinds of trials, and you know how I got out of 'em? Cause somebody prayed for me. [Thank you Jesus, sweet Jesus Lord.] That's why I'm here today. I didn't know how to pray, but somebody prayed for me. [Amen! Thank you, Lord!] I know somebody who can do anything—I'm talking about JESUS. If your God is dead, try mine. The one I'm talking about, he's my bright morning star. . . .

A bass guitar drums the air, a piano chimes in, a soloist starts to sing on the side, and the preacher asks:

Does anybody want to get religion today?

JoeAnn never understood what it meant to "get religion," but she liked everything about camp meeting. Everyone brought food to share in the food tent, and there was always plenty of fried chicken and fried catfish. The Love Feast at ten o'clock on Sunday morning was a sacred time for everyone, and almost impossible to describe to someone who hasn't been there. Perhaps those who have felt the heavy weight of oppression have a deeper bond than people who haven't. But the Love Feast was a special kind of communion shared by quietly passing a loaf of bread. Each person took a pinch and gave it to the person next to them, saying, "God has done this for me, and He has done this for you too."

When Dyke Jr. and Lula were in high school and JoeAnn was reaching her teens, they were all strong, hearty, and motivated to earn spending money. Around the farm, they wore the clothes Ora Mae made—overalls and thin cotton shirts that bore signs of heavy use—but the teenagers wanted to buy nicer outfits. DeLoach allowed them to pick peas and beans to sell at the market. The market was a social time, when other folks in the community all worked together for a little extra money. JoeAnn and her siblings liked being industrious, having spending money, and wearing store-bought clothes. Besides, it eased the burden on Ora Mae.

By the time JoeAnn was a senior in high school, her older sister and brother had graduated, and DeLoach was in his late seventies. JoeAnn could clearly see that he found the hardest farm chores nearly insurmountable. She knew he didn't want his kids involved in farm labor, but she overrode his longstanding rule the day she saw that DeLoach was feeling sickly, and the feed corn was past due for picking. The animals would need it for winter sustenance when the grassy fields died back. She hitched DeLoach's faithful horse to the handmade wagon, yelled, "Giddyap!" and steered Old Dan out into the field. For most of the day, she handpicked ears of feed corn, loaded up the wagon and commanded the horse to haul it into the barn. She felt good, she felt useful, she felt confident. In one small way she had been able to give something back to this man she called her father for his many years of selfless devotion to the family.

The summer of 1962 found JoeAnn bobbing along in an old pick-up truck and giving thanks for the opportunity to go to college. She had earned a work-study scholarship to Prentiss Institute, a college established especially for black students. She would be helping in the kitchen at mealtimes, cleaning the kitchen and dining room after meals, cleaning dorms, basically doing whatever was asked of her. Although she wasn't sure how she would fare in college, she knew it was time to leave the farm.

On one side of her sat Ora Mae, who was both proud and sad to be sending her daughter off. In the driver's seat was a friend of the family. For the first dozen miles or so it was quiet in the truck cab as they rambled along the state road from Lucedale toward the town of Natchez and the Mississippi River, four hundred miles west. Then the driver spoke. "I thought we'd pass the time telling how it came to be that black folk had their own colleges. I want to be sure this child knows what Homer Plessy did on a hot day in 1892. He is the reason that Prentiss exists."

Homer Plessy could have passed for white, his African American blood mingled with a Cajun-French medley common in Louisiana. Not only did he consider himself black, but he also had strong feelings about the law Louisiana had just passed that made it illegal for a person of color to sit in the railroad passenger cars reserved for white people. Backed by a civil rights group, he sat in a "whites only" railroad car, was arrested, and saw his case go all the way to the United States Supreme Court.

The grief and sense of loss from the Civil War was fresh in the hearts of many Southerners. The Thirteenth Amendment of 1865 had outlawed slavery; the Fourteenth had declared that state and local governments could not deprive a citizen of life, liberty, or property without certain steps being taken to ensure fairness. The Court decided in the case of Plessy v. Ferguson that separating the races did not violate the Fourteenth Amendment. Whites could have facilities separate from people of color. Blacks could have "separate but equal" facilities. Supporters of equal rights were, here and there, able to persuade financiers and land grantors to make provisions for black schools. Against the odds, black colleges and universities came into existence.

Prentiss Institute in Jefferson Davis County, Mississippi, was a year-round high school and junior college. The campus spread across many acres: enrollment was seven hundred with a faculty of forty-four. JoeAnn was somewhat baffled by it all. She was unprepared for both the social environment and the educational rigors.

Privately, JoeAnn worried that the lack of school books in the past meant that now she had the equivalent of a seventh-grade education at best. Moreover, whenever she sat in class she felt a tugging in a different direction. Two young recruiters from the Nazarene Bible Institute visited and filled her with wonder at their stories of Jesus. "He has done so much for me," one man said, and described how his life had turned around. "Whenever I have been in need, He has been there with His love," the other man said.

She wondered what use God had for a plain, black, unsophisticated small-town girl. In time, an idea rose in her mind: maybe He doesn't need me—maybe I need him.

The young men came again, and JoeAnn found herself irritated when they asked her why she was rejecting Christ. "Rejecting Christ? I don't know what you're talking about. All I know is you're trying to force something on me."

In bed that night mulling it over, she reasoned, "I'm not hungry, and I'm not sick. I'm not a 'bad' person, I haven't done anything to anger God. What would God want with me? What use is all this?" But her questions would not go away. She found herself wondering, "What does it mean to be 'called' by the Lord? What does it mean to be Christian?" Slowly, she began to feel a little light growing inside. She was interested in the Bible college in West Virginia that she had heard was integrated. She continued attending classes at Prentiss but began to ask more questions of the Nazarene evangelists when they came to visit.

By that fall she had had enough of secular education and wrote her mother: "Come and get me in two weeks. I'm going to Bible college." JoeAnn set to work applying for enrollment and scholarships at the Nazarene Bible Institute, and the Nazarenes gave her a partial work scholarship. Saying her good-byes and apologies around Prentiss, she told people: "I'm going to do something for God. I don't know what—but something."

She gathered her things, and on the appointed day waited for her daddy's beat-up Dodge farm truck to come around the bend.

Ora Mae's face was emotional as she stepped down from the truck. She put her hands on each side of JoeAnn's face and said, "Child, you know you can't make any money as a preacher."

While they hadn't seen it coming, neither Ora Mae nor the rest of the family were surprised. JoeAnn was known as "a good girl" who stayed close to home, went to church with her family most Sundays, and didn't drink, smoke, or do things that were considered immoral for an unmarried female. Young JoeAnn hoped the Nazarene Bible Institute could offer her spiritual growth and nurture, and she reasoned that it was racially integrated and seemed like a safe place to explore her newfound religious questions.

Back home in Lucedale, DeLoach sat in the passenger's seat of his recently acquired old Dodge truck and taught JoeAnn to drive. She was a quick learner and earned her license within a month.

By mid-September, cotton-picking time was at hand. The long rows of thigh-high plants had dropped their leaves, leaving only the bolls: the dark, hardened fingers of the plant holding its seed to the sky. Historically, slaves (and barely paid black farm workers after them) were not provided protective gear and suffered silently the painful process of battling the razor-sharp edges of each boll that curled protectively around its precious white plume.

Temperatures at cotton-picking time soared near 100 degrees at midday, so JoeAnn tried to get out at dawn like the other farmhands, before the sun could heat up the fields. She wore long sleeves despite the heat, trying to shield her arms from the torturous scratches. Carrying an eight-foot-long burlap sack with a long shoulder strap, she worked over the short plants all day long. At the end of the week her back ached like never before, and her hands and arms were sliced and scratched. By the end of the month, she had handpicked enough cotton to buy the bus tickets that would take her to the small Bible college tucked away in a rocky corner of West Virginia.

"Here, honey."

Ora Mae—Momma—handed her daughter a neatly folded

batch of blouses, skirts, sheets, and pillowcases, all fashioned and sewn, stitch by stitch, with her own loving hands. Over the past two weeks she had poured her breaking heart into sewing while JoeAnn had picked cotton. The only store-bought items in Joe-Ann's large wooden footlocker were her socks, underpants, and bra. Oh, yes, and an overcoat. Ora Mae was fervent that her baby girl be warm in the approaching West Virginia winter. Growing up thirty miles from the tropical Gulf Coast, JoeAnn had seen snow only once in her life.

Hugging her daughter good-bye at the Gulf gas station— which served as a bus terminal for Lucedale folk—Ora Mae closed her eyes. Eighteen years of memories flooded past: feeding, dressing, teaching, and protecting this beautiful child. "You've grown into a strong young woman," she breathed, barely able to inhale. "This is your time to shine, honey."

JoeAnn swallowed her own emotions until she was on the bus. With the bus roaring onto the state road, JoeAnn watched as Ora Mae looked smaller and smaller through the window. Then, and only then, did JoeAnn's tears come.

From Lucedale through the Great Smoky Mountains to West Virginia, a series of buses carried JoeAnn more than eight hundred miles northeast. In the town of Laurel, Mississippi, she was joined by four other students she had known at Prentiss who were also headed to the Bible Institute. Two were the Walker brothers, along with Charles "Stick" Jones, and Edward Husband, who would turn out to be a powerful minister. The four young men were her protectors as well as friends of the family. When they got hungry, JoeAnn happily shared her food with them. From the paper bags her momma had prepared she pulled out various delights. First came fried chicken and home-cured ham sandwiches, then cheese and biscuits and cake. All she had to buy was a cold drink now and then. A day or so later she missed her momma's cooking like never before.

Passing the Mississippi state line, she remembered a troubling news headline she had seen at the gas station. It was about James Meredith, a young black man who was denied admission to the all-white University of Mississippi. John F. Kennedy, the president of the United States, sent U.S. marshals to accompany and protect Meredith as he attempted to come on campus on October 1, 1962. Getting off the bus in Birmingham to wait for the next bus east, JoeAnn could feel the tension in the air. "They closed the parks," said a lady sitting next to her. "My boy got his nose broken when the police turned fire hoses on him and his friends."

Faced with integration, white authorities in Birmingham had closed its public parks and public golf courses rather than let black people use them or protest on them. Black people who dared to peacefully protest in the South were freely harassed and beaten by local police wielding oak nightsticks. They turned dangerously powerful water hoses on the protesters, knocking them down and sending them sprawling. They also brought terrifying German shepherd police dogs, trained to attack.

On each bus JoeAnn asked the white driver—with utmost politeness—"I'm headed to Charleston, West Virginia; please make sure I get off at the right place." Barreling down state roads, she watched the towns go by, noticing how they were mostly similar and the few ways they were different. Through Chattanooga, past Knoxville, the bus wrenched toward the Great Smoky Mountains and the Cherokee National Forest. The driver barely slowed down on the curving, winding roads that poured across the mountainsides. When he did hit the brakes, it was a frightening jolt for eighteen-year-old JoeAnn.

It was morning when they pulled into the Charleston, West Virginia, bus terminal. JoeAnn had been traveling on buses for twenty-two hours. She was worn out but excited to be starting a new life. One of the men in her group found a pay phone and called the president of the Nazarene Bible Institute to come and get them. In no time, a long 1961 station wagon, turquoise with white-wall tires pulled up, and Rev. R. W. Cunningham stepped out to greet them. He was both the president of the college and pastor of the on-campus Church of the Nazarene.

After a short ride, they reached a stately campus, which was much larger than JoeAnn had imagined. It was the thrill of her lifetime to see young black men and women strolling among the tall brick buildings—until she realized that their car was simply driving past West Virginia State University. In the post-Reconstruction Era, it had been congressionally authorized and founded as West Virginia Colored Institute, with an instructional focus on farming and machine work.

The Nazarene Bible Institute in West Virginia was much smaller than the state university. In addition to a classroom building, there was a handsome brick administrative building and a two-story wood-frame structure where nonacademic student activities took place. Downstairs were the girls' rooms, the kitchen and dining room, and a front room that served triple duty as chapel, student activity room, and visiting parlor. Male students lived on the second floor. A separate church stood on campus a little farther down the road.

Anna Bowman, the girls' dorm mother, warmly greeted JoeAnn at the front door and led her back to the bedrooms. JoeAnn's faithful companions followed along, lugging her large footlocker. As the first girl to arrive, she had her pick of rooms. She chose the middle room with an old-fashioned double window and took a small bed by the window.

"When are the other girls coming?" she asked.

"Oh, we expect the girls to show up soon," was the answer.

In the morning JoeAnn joined a handful of boys and not a single other girl in the dining room to say grace and sit down to breakfast. Breakfast consisted of fried apples, white-bread toast, and small link sausages with very little flavor. JoeAnn wondered silently where the rest of the breakfast was. Where were the grits, ham, eggs, and coffee? The breakfast menu puzzled her since three-quarters of the people on campus were black, but JoeAnn had rarely eaten food that had not been cooked by Ora Mae. At lunchtime she discovered that the cafeteria food would always be bland and minimalist to her Mississippi taste buds. Indeed, much of the daily menu was the result of donated food. If someone showed up with a load of canned vegetables and fruit, Praise Jesus—that's what they ate that week.

Every last hope in the young girl's mind went dark when she learned that she would be the only girl on campus the entire semester. Alone in her room that night, she fell across the cotton bedspread and had a big cry. Then she marched down the hall to the pay phone and slid in enough quarters to call her mother. "It's too different from what I'm used to," she confessed. "I don't feel at home here with indoor plumbing and telephones and food that's nothing like what you cook. And I'm the only girl surrounded by twenty boys!"

Ora Mae, who had originally wanted her daughter to attend a secular school, was unmoved. The girl had picked her path, now she had to walk it. "Child, it's only been a few days. Remember what you went there for. Give it a little while longer."

The Nazarene college's mission was to spread the Good News of Jesus Christ by training ministers and sending them forth. Core doctrines of the Church of the Nazarene evolved from John Wesley's teachings and the holiness movement of the nineteenth century but with a more fundamentalist twist: there was a focus on witnessing God's work in human lives. Several denominations merged in the United States to form the Church of the Nazarene, including some Pentecostal, Evangelical, and Holiness churches. It was, and is, a predominantly white denomination.

Sometimes JoeAnn wondered what she was doing at the Bible Institute, anyway, since she was ambiguous about being in ministry and had never seen a black female minister. But life at Bible college soon became potent medicine for the Mississippi girl who was, after all, following a blind impulse to be there in the first place. The change in JoeAnn was sparked when students were summoned to Wednesday night prayer meeting at the church on campus. The program was like fresh bait thrown into the water beside a fish that had never eaten and didn't know it was hungry. Her encounter with these evangelical Christians left her spellbound. Everyone seemed "plugged in" to something . . . into the same thing.

As the choir sang in impassioned voices, a woman rose from wooden pews to follow Reverend Cunningham's call to the altar, her face alive with feeling, alive with faith. Another woman came forth and declared in resonant tones how she came to have a "personal relationship" with Jesus Christ. These words were new to JoeAnn. The testimonials came one after the other, disturbing her as much as they inspired her for they formed a fresh question, a profound inquiry, in her own heart: Do I really know Jesus Christ? Do I want to know him? With no one to talk to, no roommate, no other students at all on the downstairs floor with her, the testimonials about Jesus simmered quietly inside her for the rest of the week. Through her classes, as she walked on campus, in everything she did, the questions worked powerfully on her.

On Sunday morning JoeAnn performed the necessary hair ritual: heating an iron and pressing her hair flat, then curling it with a curling iron. She felt confident walking through the campus church in a new dress with new black patent-leather shoes. Sunday school, before the service, was similar to what she had known back at home, except for a greater reliance on the Bible. The teacher often opened his Bible and easily turned to specific passages to emphasize a point or lend authority to his message. The main church service was emotional and Spirit-filled. Few souls could resist the choir, led by a soloist whose voice was teeming with emotion as they led congregants in a plaintive, heartrending version of "Tell Jesus All." In the Nazarene hymnal underneath the song title was the Biblical reference: "Because he himself suffered . . . he is able to help." (Heb. 2:18.)

The music washed over her, the lyrics opened her: "What must

I do when worldliness calls me?" She thought of Reverend Cunningham's sermon about sin, how easy it is to fall into it, how blind we are to our own transgressions against God and against our fellow men. The soloist confessed in the lyrics of the song: "I must tell Jesus all of my trials. I cannot bear these burdens alone. . . ."

"You know what's in your heart," Reverend Cunningham said, his voice big and bold. "If you have a sadness, if you have a hunger, if you have a need, come on up, come forward to the altar."

JoeAnn shut her eyes tight and gripped the wooden pew underneath her. *I can't. I know I am a sinner but . . . Lord, I'm not ready for . . . whatever this is,* she told herself.

She returned to the dorm without telling anyone of her deepening struggle. Within a few weeks she was sure that she was a sinner in need of salvation. She wrote in her journal: "I cannot stand myself. But I do not want anyone to know that I need God. I guess that is my pride." Young JoeAnn found herself preparing inwardly to give her life to God, to summon all that she had and yield it to the Great Almighty. By the time a Wednesday night service rolled around in early October, she knew it was her time. As a choir of voices filled the church in confessional arias, JoeAnn strode to the altar. "I know I am a sinner," she began, and when Reverend Cunningham asked the ultimate question, she uttered the Christian pledge with every ounce of her being. "I accept Jesus Christ as my personal Savior." She felt cleansed. She felt brand new. She had been born again.

Snow began to fall in late October, bringing down the last autumn leaves and cloaking the campus in white. Without telephones, without television or access to outside news other than what Reverend Cunningham brought them, there were no distractions for the students at Nazarene Bible Institute. Cunningham and his wife were models of quiet diligence, living examples of selfless service. They gave and gave to the community and always had more to give. The Cunninghams were assisted by another husband-and-wife team, Rev. and Mrs. Clarence Bowman, who lived with their two small children in an apartment adjacent to the dorm.

Before the students had risen from bed or had the first thought about sitting down to the family-style breakfast, Reverend Cunningham had already checked the kitchen pantry to be sure there was enough food for that day's meals and that the kitchen helpers were beginning their duties. When supplies were needed for the students or his own house, he personally drove the twenty-four miles to Charleston and back. He not only knew the names of every student but also of every person in the neighboring community and greeted them with a smile and a tip of his hat as he passed. He ran the school, led religious services on Sunday mornings and Wednesdays, and on Thursday nights he taught classes. Although the textbooks were woefully outdated, he made the material come alive, speaking enthusiastically and tying the institute's studies into current events. "He sees the best in us," JoeAnn thought, watching him. Besides tending to fifty or sixty students and a handful of teachers and staff, Cunningham was a devoted husband and father who enjoyed working in his yard and tending his goldfish pond.

Mrs. Cunningham seemed to pray all day and all night. She prayed for every need that reached her ears. She prayed for people's bodies as well as their souls. She prayed for relief from their suffering, for peace among family members and between enemies, for folks to find a job. When JoeAnn came to her for counseling, she sat knee to knee holding hands with JoeAnn and prayed for guidance. "Lord, You know Your daughter here before You. You can see that her will, her life, is open to Your direction. We know, Lord Jesus, with confident hearts that You are already preparing the place where Miss JoeAnn can serve you best."

JoeAnn joined the Nazarene Young People's Society and enjoyed its weekly meetings at the Nazarene church. Classroom instruction was more evangelistic now, shifting away from one's inner journey and moving toward ministry training, with classes like "The Art of Soul Winning." She was determined to win some souls for Jesus—and where better to start than her own family?

Each week JoeAnn wrote her parents back home and her brother, Dyke, at Alcorn College. "I've been saved," she wrote, "I have found this precious jewel, Jesus, and I want you to know Him too." On visits home, JoeAnn carried her Bible around the house and sometimes read aloud to her parents. She wanted the family to go to church together three nights a week; she wanted to visit the sick and elderly of Lucedale. At every turn, JoeAnn offered suggestions to her family about how they could turn their lives over to Jesus.

The idea of ministering to people made JoeAnn shimmer with excitement. It would be something of an uphill climb since at that time ministers were almost always men. But as far back as 1902, the Nazarene church had trained women as pastors and lay leaders. Women—but white women. As a black female minister, Joe-Ann would be an unusual creature by anybody's standards. Constantly unsure how to use her ministry training, JoeAnn asked, deeply, "What are all the ways I can serve God's people?

Her enthusiasm for Christ eventually spread to her brother because not long after she returned from a visit home, she was called to the dorm's pay phone. It was Dyke: "Get ready 'cause here I come for the winter semester! I'll be there in a few days." Dyke had become a Christian. Furthermore, he'd heard the call to become a preacher.

College life became brighter with JoeAnn's big brother on campus. Her spirits also improved when two new girls joined her in the dorm. They became instant friends. The three of them often sat up late in the night, holding their pillows in their laps and talking about boys, God, and school. The other girls weren't studying to be pastors, and by the spring, they had boyfriends.

The students' lives were as cloistered as the school itself, hidden away in the granite mountains of southern Appalachia. The boys earned spending money in low-paying part-time jobs at the

Union Carbide manufacturing facility in South Charleston. The girls were hired to babysit for local families. As a special treat, the boys would walk a little ways down the road to West Virginia State University and order bologna sandwiches at the grill. Since the institute's cafeteria menu was sparse on beef, pork, and animal fat in general, a fried bologna sandwich on white bread slathered with mayonnaise was a special treat. If they had an extra dime, they'd also get a Coca-Cola.

Dyke had gotten a job at the local Shoney's Big Boy and one day convinced his manager to let the girls from the Nazarene Bible Institute, all three of them, come and eat for free. The girls were delighted and put on the best clothes they owned. They couldn't have dressed any better if they'd been heading out to a four-star restaurant. Dyke made sure they were treated like special guests and gave them extra-large helpings of French fries and a free drink refill.

JoeAnn's first year at Bible college had been wonderful, and she looked forward to the coming school year. But she needed to earn money to pay for it. Fortunately an opportunity arose for her to spend the summer of 1963 in New York City with her godmother, Florence Jones, so she made her way north for a new adventure.

She awoke at sunrise that first morning in New York to find that her godmother had gone to work, so JoeAnn set out on foot to find a job. After five hours of hunting combined with a bit of sightseeing, she found a factory in the garment district that was looking to hire additional help. She had found herself a summer job—joining dozens of other women sitting in rows bent over sewing machines—to help pay for the coming year of school. While she would always love the peace and quiet of the country, as the weeks went on, she found herself energized by the hustle and bustle of New York and wondered if she would someday end up in a big city.

When the new school year started, JoeAnn spent more time in prayer while other young women were finding husbands. Couples, including JoeAnn's brother, Dyke, and his girlfriend, made plans for marriage. JoeAnn was still unattached and unsure of what to do after graduation. She felt the call to ministry—but not the call to preach. Although in due course she could easily preach and testify to the Holy Spirit moving in people's lives, her call was in working with people, performing the work of the church in the field, not from the pulpit.

Her parents' constant devotion to the children who were not their own and the community at large had ignited in JoeAnn a deep need to nourish others. She wrestled with the question of how to serve and looked to the Bible for resolution. An answer came one day while reading Isaiah 40:31: "But they that wait upon the Lord shall renew their strength . . . they shall run, and not be weary. . . ." A state of calm came over her, and although she still had no specific direction, she felt inwardly reassured that she was on the right path.

That Christmas JoeAnn boarded the bus and went home for vacation. This time, however, she was not required to sit in the back, countering the longstanding custom in the South. She set herself down in the front of the bus, smoothed out the lap of her skirt, and took in the view. *Goodness,* she thought to herself, *from here, you can look down at everything!* When she had first gone to college in 1962, she knew better than to try to sit in the front on that long, twenty-two-hour journey. In some ways, things had gotten worse since then. The Ku Klux Klan had murdered prominent black Mississippian Medgar Evers, the field secretary for the NAACP (National Association of the Advancement of Colored People). He was shot down in front of his own house as he emerged from his car after driving home. Elsewhere, armed Klansmen assaulted members of black churches across the South, burning their houses of worship to the ground and killing and injuring innocent men, women, and children.

JoeAnn wanted to believe that things in the South were changing, if only a little. Dr. Martin Luther King Jr.'s searing speeches

42

and writings were opening the eyes and hearts of many Americans. He had been arrested in Birmingham for "parading without a permit" while protesting segregation. On the fourth day behind those iron bars, King wrote of his heartbreak over the contemporary church, calling it "a weak, ineffectual voice with an uncertain sound. . . . If today's church does not recapture the sacrificial spirit of the early church, it will lose its authenticity, forfeit the loyalty of millions, and be dismissed as an irrelevant social club with no meaning for the twentieth century."

As the school year pushed toward conclusion, JoeAnn continuously pondered three questions: What is the role of the church today? What does the life of a Christian look like? What am I going to do after college? A few weeks before graduation, JoeAnn planted herself in the middle of the administration building steps so as not to be overlooked by Elder Warren Rogers Sr., who was visiting the campus. As district superintendent of the Church of the Nazarene Gulf Central District, he oversaw all the black congregations in the Nazarene Church in the United States.

"Young lady, are you ready for the future?"

"Yes, sir." Her voice would not rise to full volume.

"How would you like to go to Memphis, Tennessee, and start a Sunday school in a neighborhood there?"

Her heart leaped nearly out of her chest. "Yes, sir!"

"Meet me Tuesday at nine o'clock sharp. I'll get you a car, paid for by a generous Nazarene layman."

She could feel his hand gently pat her back as he turned down the steps, but she could barely take in the impact of his words. *I am going to Memphis! To start a Sunday school class! And I am getting a car!* Her wondering and worrying about the future was over at last. The future had arrived.

∼THREE∼
Memphis and Marriage

THE KENTUCKY CAR DEALER WHO HAD PLEDGED
to give a car to a Nazarene Bible Institute graduate headed
for the ministry may have been surprised when the student turned
out to be a young woman headed to revive a Sunday school instead
of a young man headed to the pulpit. But he made good on the
promise, and when JoeAnn graduated in 1965, she was given a
1956 Oldsmobile—the best-looking car in America when it first
came out. It was two-toned blue and white, with a V-8 engine
and two hundred horsepower under the hood. Voluptuous fenders
flanked a large grille below the rounded hood.

"I'll drive. You just look around and enjoy the ride," her brother
Dyke told her.

Having a car was a privilege, and JoeAnn's mouth trembled a
little as she recalled that her family's lack of a car at the time was
the reason her sister, Lula, became permanently brain damaged. A
lively, quick-witted girl, smart and confident, Lula always brought
home straight As from school. Until she got sick. At first it seemed
like just a bad cold that wouldn't go away. Then Ora Mae realized
that the monster that had wrapped itself around her daughter's
lungs was pneumonia. With no phone in the house and no car,
DeLoach rode his horse, Old Dan, to their neighbor's house to
ask them to fetch the doctor fast. But Lula's fever stayed too high
for too long, and by the time the doctor came the next day, the
damage was done. After that it seemed as if Lula couldn't make
good decisions like she had in the past. She couldn't bring success
into her life. Forever after, JoeAnn tended to Lula from afar. Often she found herself doing something in Lula's name, dedicating

44

herself to her sister, and rededicating herself to God.

As the outskirts of Memphis came into view, JoeAnn saw the broad Mississippi River that separated Tennessee from Arkansas gliding southward alongside them.

"They carried slaves on that river," her brother said, unflinching.

For thousands of years, the ancient Mississippi has carried dreams and debris down from Minnesota to the Gulf of Mexico. Like a turtle, it is generally in no hurry, sliding along so slowly that the average person can outpace it. But the river is mighty, drawing into itself countless streams and tributaries, beckoning rainfall and snowmelts from more than half the land in the United States as well as Canada. Rainfall anywhere north of Memphis can swell its banks to devastating proportions. Gentle as a young girl's smile one day and as vengeful as a wounded warrior the next, the Mississippi is a force to be reckoned with. JoeAnn felt its silent power and nodded.

Then, around a bend, stood the city. JoeAnn drew in a sharp breath. Nearly half a million people lived in Memphis in 1965. Outside of her brief summer stint spent in New York City, twenty-one-year-old JoeAnn had never seen anything like it. Her life had bloomed on the family farm in Mississippi and stretched out in the prayerful days and nights of Bible college in West Virginia.

Over a century earlier, Memphis had become the slave-trading center of the mid-South despite the large number of state societies opposed to it. In the face of abolitionist pressure, some people began freeing their slaves in the 1830s. Freed slaves in Tennessee, like JoeAnn's great-uncle Dan Lawrence, were granted important privileges. They could attend private schools in Memphis and Nashville, receive religious instruction, enter into contracts, and inherit—but not buy—property. But laws on the books don't change people's hearts, and freed slaves were often viewed like inmates on parole. Abolitionists and slave owners battled each other in the legislature, in courts, and on the streets while the slave trade soared.

In the long state of Tennessee, white people were utterly divided on the slavery issue, with lines drawn based on farming economics. In the east, where farms were small and the land and climate did not favor cotton, people sided with the Union. In western Tennessee and the Mississippi Delta, where the world's primary supply of cotton was grown by slave labor, people favored seceding from the Union. As one plantation owner said, "I've got to buy more Negroes to raise more cotton to buy more Negroes to raise more cotton." The 1840 census showed 183,000 Negro slaves in Tennessee, most of them working in the cotton fields in the western part of the state.

If JoeAnn had been able to see through time by squinting at the river, she might have seen the 1862 Battle of Memphis, witnessed by virtually everyone in town. It was, like much of the Civil War, a crushing defeat for the South. With no time to build warships, each side quickly commandeered whatever was already floating. In the North, where manufacturing was already in swing, most vessels were iron-clad or tin-clad. The South's navy consisted of riverboats clad in the only resources at hand, timber and cotton—the "cottonclads" weren't actually clad in cotton but rather the bales lined the wooden ships' sides to protect them from enemy fire—and were commanded by riverboat captains who knew nothing of war. The people of Memphis stood on the Chickasaw bluffs and watched Union ships annihilate the CSS *General Beauregard* and the rest of the Rebel fleet.

After the Emancipation Proclamation of 1863, thousands of black people left the rural South for the cities of the North, hoping to find jobs, housing, a new life. Many of them walked hundreds of miles. Although the Memphis and Charleston Railroad had been completed in 1857, it was both expensive and off-limits to any black people who weren't employed on the train serving food or working as porters.

As the South's cities struggled to reconstruct after the Civil War, the reappearance of yellow fever brought a black majority population in Memphis for the first time. The city had been exposed to the highly contagious disease three times previously: 1828, 1855, and 1867, each time brought by a steamer from New Orleans.

When a few physicians began reporting in 1878 that the deadly disease had returned, a mass exodus began. More than half of its 45,000 citizens fled any way they could, but neighboring towns issued quarantines and refused Memphis's citizens entrance. Churches became makeshift hospitals filled with patients suffering from black vomit, fever, chills, and jaundiced skin.

African Americans, recently freed from slavery, had neither the means nor the money to leave. As luck would have it—some said it was God's mercy—something in their African ancestry graced many of them with a measure of protection against yellow fever. Of the five thousand white people who stayed behind, only one thousand lived. Of the fourteen thousand black people who remained, thirteen thousand survived. They sang and prayed and nursed each other through it.

The next century saw Memphis waiting out the Great Depression of 1929. It had been the center of trade and commerce for long enough that it did not bottom out in the coming years. Nevertheless, white people now found themselves competing for many of the same jobs—cleaning, driving, short-order cooking—that had historically been filled by black people.

Down on Beale Street, blues, jazz, and gospel music rocked the streets, beginning around 1910 with the songs of the "Father of the Blues," African American composer W. C. Handy. By the early 1950s, Sun Records Studio producer Sam Phillips was recording Elvis Presley, Jerry Lee Lewis, Roy Orbison, Carl Perkins, and Johnny Cash. A spunky musician who called himself Blues Boy King hitchhiked to town and become a regular on Beale Street. As his fame grew, he shortened his name to B. B. King.

JoeAnn arrived in Memphis in May 1965. At first the city seemed wild. The loudness of it, the rhythm and blues in the

47

bones of its buildings, the urban-meets-rural landscape—it was too much for the young woman to take in. The redbrick buildings on Beale Street had long been fertile ground for traveling blues players who played their souls right out into the air night after night. Their sensuous notes beguiled white customers to cross the racial line and sit down and have a few drinks. Jazz, blues, and liquor seeded radio stations that magnetized more talent to town. Beale Street was, as radio announcer Nat D. Williams observed, "a spirit . . . a symbol . . . a way of life. . . . Beale Street is a hope." But the noise and bright lights were only masking the darkness.

The summer before, three civil rights workers (two white, one black) who had been attempting to register black voters in Mississippi were beaten, lynched, shot, and buried in an earthen dam. The Civil Rights Act of July 1964, attempted—and failed—to protect women, religious minorities, and ethnic groups from overt discrimination. Bigotry ruled. In every public arena, from restaurants to drinking fountains, black people were barred from using the same facilities as whites.

Back in JoeAnn's hometown, black people knew better than to endanger their families' safety by trying to get to the polls. Fully 98 percent of George County voters chose George Wallace in the upcoming presidential election. It is safe to say they were all white racists. Wallace, elected governor of Alabama four times beginning in 1963, once told the *New York Times* that integration should be stopped, and all that was needed to stop integration was a "few first-class funerals."

JoeAnn remembered Emmett Till, the fourteen-year-old who was murdered and thrown off a Mississippi bridge in 1955. Two white men kidnapped the boy in the middle of the night, beat him, gouged out one of his eyes, and shot him through the head. They then wrapped barbed wire around his body, attaching it to a heavy cotton-gin fan, and pushed it off a bridge into the Tallahatchie River. JoeAnn couldn't stop the fear coming into her heart as she wondered if her brother would be next. Not because he had done anything wrong, but simply because he was a Negro boy. Every time her brother went out of her sight, she worried that he would be killed. Whenever he left her, she would warn him, "Don't you say anything to any white folks at all." JoeAnn's brother gave her a talk as well about staying safe and not taking chances with white people as she dropped him off at the bus station to head back to Charleston and the Nazarene Bible Institute.

Even with all the tension, Memphis seemed like a place where a black person might have a chance. Before the successful musicians and recording artists of the 1940s, '50s, and '60s, there had been a handful of prominent black businessmen, including R. R. Church, a real-estate mogul and America's first black millionaire. Filled with both a healthy dose of fear and an even larger one of hope, JoeAnn set out to make the city her home.

A local Nazarene pastor and his wife had agreed to rent her a room in their modest brick home. The pastor's wife treated Joe-Ann kindly, in the manner one would expect from a southern preacher's wife. The reverend was in charge of a church in another part of town and stayed busy with his duties and congregants.

JoeAnn's monthly budget was eighty-five dollars. With that, she needed to pay the forty dollars rent, feed herself for thirty days, take care of car insurance and gas expenses, and buy everything needed to jump-start a Sunday school in a closed-down church. But this was a girl who knew how to scrimp and save, make do, and do without.

Her first morning in Memphis, JoeAnn put on her best dress, freshly pressed, and headed to the bank. The Nazarene church had given her a check for five hundred dollars—her entire budget for the summer. Driving up to the first bank she saw, she parked, went inside, and walked to a clerk's desk.

"I need to make a deposit," she said.

The woman behind the desk regarded her quizzically. "Please, have a seat." Then, giving JoeAnn a gentle look, she asked, "I'm sorry, but I need to ask: what is the amount you will be depositing?

"Five hundred dollars."

"Just a moment, please." The clerk walked across the room and disappeared behind a closed door. JoeAnn had to wonder if this was all because she was young and black. A different woman emerged, wearing a crisp suit and heels, and introduced herself.

"Ma'am, I regret to tell you that this is not the kind of bank you need. This is a Federal Reserve Bank. The deposits at this bank start at ten thousand dollars."

JoeAnn realized she had a lot to learn about living on her own in a big city.

Driving on busy Memphis streets was unnerving. By contrast, Lucedale had a single stoplight. JoeAnn had never driven a car in traffic. It was summer, the car had no air conditioner, and in the southern heat, she sweated profusely—both from nerves and temperature—whenever she drove. One day as a summer rain poured down, steaming up the car windows, she stopped at a light waiting to turn left across rush-hour traffic. The rain came in torrents, making it hard for her to see. JoeAnn waited for a green light to tell her she could turn left, but there didn't seem to be one. The light stayed red. Meanwhile, cars began stacking in a line behind her. Someone honked. More cars piled up and honked. The line behind her was so long, she couldn't see the end of it in her rearview mirror. Then came a rap on her window. She rolled it down.

"Ma'am," the man yelled through the rain, "look at the bottom of the red light. There's a green arrow that pops up. When you see that green arrow, turn left!"

Grateful to the man for his help, she nodded and watched carefully for that green arrow.

The next day, she pulled on the one pair of overalls she owned and drove out to 1868 Castex Street in South Memphis. She thought of the instructions in the letter from the Nazarene Gulf Coast District: "Revive the Sunday school program." The church's pastor had resigned more than a year earlier, and the already dwindling congregation had just stayed home after that. It was less than five miles down East McLemore Avenue, over the expressway that would later be renamed for Dr. King, to the Riverview district. Just a few blocks from the Mississippi, it had once been a stable black neighborhood with a mixture of rental properties and homeowners, mostly black. But as the older generation died off, the neighborhood had steadily fallen into decline.

Anybody who cared to look would have noticed a pretty young girl involuntarily drawing in a deep breath when she pulled up alongside the Memphis South Church of the Nazarene. It looked like a haunted house standing in a graveyard. The lawn had been let go, and weeds had taken over; the one-story building had been shut tight for more than a year, and paint peeled off the asbestos siding in so many places, it gave a pockmarked effect. And something smelled dead and rotten.

Picking up a fallen branch, she used it to clear a veil of cobwebs that stood between her and the front door. Stirring the air with the stick as silvery strands grabbed hold, JoeAnn couldn't help but smile as she remembered DeLoach's magic bandage. She was only eight at the time, trying to help Dyke cut up a fresh-killed chicken for dinner. Pressing too hard too quickly, she had run the knife into her forefinger almost to the bone.

"Daddy! Daddy! JoeAnn cut her finger!" Dyke yelled.

DeLoach was there in a heartbeat, one hand covered in white silky threads. Wrapping them around his daughter's finger, he spoke in calm tones and reassured her, "This will stop the bleeding and help it mend, Fannie. Don't you worry."

When JoeAnn made her way inside the dilapidated church, the sheetrock ceiling told the tale of repeated water leaks, and one corner of the floor was damp. Without hesitation, she rolled up her sleeves, pulled cleaning supplies from her car, and set to work. Every day for six weeks, she scraped, scrubbed, swept, pruned, scythed, and raked. She went to the hardware store nearby and talked the owner into giving her a five-gallon bucket of whitewash, promising that it would help to improve the neighborhood, and started brightening up the outside of the church. Folks from the neighborhood walked by and took long looks. Sometimes Joe-Ann took a little break to be friendly and explain what she was doing. She thought it odd that no one came to pitch in, to work alongside her. Instead, she was met with disbelief: "They sent *you*?" one woman asked.

Finally JoeAnn had the place as clean as it was ever going to get, the yard in order, and a few Sunday-school supplies in the classroom. She had a snack of orange juice and graham crackers to give the many kids she was expecting. Climbing into bed Saturday night, she felt ready—mostly. Everything she was doing, she was doing for the first time, making it up as she went along. She had never taught Sunday school, either. But each day before she got out of bed, she dug down deep and asked, "What has God put in me that I can use to help people?"

Sunday morning she buttoned up her blue gabardine dress and arrived at the church two hours early. It was late July, and the air was warm and clammy inside the church building as she waited. Nine o'clock, nine-thirty, ten . . . not a single child came. Or parents. No children, no men, no women. Nobody. At ten-thirty, Joe-Ann headed out to the First Church of the Nazarene for comfort.

After church, JoeAnn had a new perspective. "I've got to start over. I need to make fliers. I need to make this look more official." Women at the First Church of the Nazarene helped JoeAnn craft the message and hand-cranked purple-ink papers through a mimeograph machine. "I'm not a quitter," she told herself aloud, driving down the road with a stack of notices. She taped them all over the neighborhood: at a drugstore, a beauty salon, a snack bar. She went house to house, chatting with people and making sure they knew there would be Sunday school in the Memphis South Church of the Nazarene every week at nine in the morning.

The following Sunday she put on the same dress—since no one had seen it yet—and waited inside the church. Not a soul came. She tried the next Sunday; same thing. Each Sunday she waited alone, then drove to a different church to explore the local offerings.

In her weariness and discouragement, she once again turned to the same passage in the book of Isaiah that had encouraged her in Bible college: *"But they that wait upon the Lord . . . shall mount up with wings as eagles; they shall run, and not be weary; and they shall walk, and not faint."*

As she clung to her faith for continued strength and guidance, one day, it hit her: *People need a reason to come.* She had to offer something more than the idea of Sunday school. *Why would they just show up when they don't know me, and I don't know them or what their lives are like?* She understood that she did not know what others had been through. And not knowing their life experiences, she could not know what their needs were.

It was a life-changing moment and one that put her decades ahead of the anti-poverty movement in America. One hundred thousand black people lived in Memphis, half of those in poverty. It was JoeAnn's first encounter with people whose main self-identity was "poor." JoeAnn also learned that people can't be helped unless they want to be helped and unless they have been truly engaged in relationship.

But for true relating to take place, those providing help must give up seeing themselves as "helpers" and stop seeing other people as "recipients." Anything done through the perspective of helper-receiver only serves to reinforce the disparity of roles, and the perceived disparity sucks the life out of people who need help.

The way JoeAnn saw it, the helper-receiver perspective was just one more type of enslavement. From the Christian perspective, JoeAnn was learning that the goal of service is not just to bring people to church but rather to *be* the church.

As the whole picture became clear to her, she shook her head at the simplicity of it all, the profoundness of it all, and said silently, *Carrying this out is going to take the rest of my life.*

She held the new illumination in her heart as she once again went door to door to the homes and apartments within a mile radius of the church. This time she brought a three-question survey and a humble introduction. "I want to start a Sunday school at the Nazarene church," she'd say, "but first I need to know: Do you have a home church? Would you like to attend and send your kids to Sunday school? If so, what would it take to get you to church?" She found folks hungry to talk about their lives, willing to confide that the main reason they didn't send their children or go themselves to the church on Sunday was because they didn't have any decent clothes. Everybody wanted to look nice in the House of the Lord.

Armed with new knowledge, JoeAnn took up the challenge. She gathered their names, sizes, and the type of clothing they needed and prayed that God would help her find clothes for them all. It was true that these people didn't have money for clothes—but neither did JoeAnn, with her eighty-dollar monthly budget. She took the five dollars left over from her monthly allowance, slipped into the Olds, and ventured a little ways out of the neighborhood—something she did not like to do as she was still terrified of driving in heavy city traffic.

Turning a corner, two shops came into view, across the street from one another, their names shining like beacons from above: "Salvation Army" and "Goodwill." Shirts and skirts were only ten cents each, enabling JoeAnn to buy armloads of clothes for her five-dollar budget. Giving out the clothes in the neighborhood that week, she felt more like an apprentice than a provider. She was keenly aware that these people had something to teach her. She just didn't know what it was yet.

The following Sunday morning, JoeAnn waited in the doorway of the little church that had stood quiet for more than a year. She couldn't help but smile at the small group of diverse children headed her way. It had been twelve weeks since JoeAnn arrived and began refurbishing the church, twelve weeks of sweat and trial and error. But here they came: ten children, the older ones leading the smaller ones, plus a young mother carrying her infant and his baby bottle. Sunday school was finally in session at the Memphis South Church of the Nazarene.

JoeAnn visited neighborhood homes and bought clothes for those in need several more times. Soon the needs exceeded her budget, but by then those involved became inspired to buy their own Goodwill and Salvation Army clothes and seemed to enjoy spending Sunday mornings together.

On her own for the first time in her life, JoeAnn found a level of faith that never would have been accessible if she were still in the nest of her parents' farm or the sheltered campus of the Nazarene Bible Institute. Living with the pastor and his wife provided home base—and then one day he suddenly announced that JoeAnn had to move out. No reason was given, and she never understood why. Coming from a tight-knit Christian community in rural Mississippi, the minister's announcement marked the first time she ever felt betrayed by someone she deeply trusted. There had always been surprises and a certain amount of letdowns, but to be put out on the street by another Christian was a kick in the gut.

Stunned at this news, she set out on foot, hoping the walk would calm her. Her thoughts ran hot and cold. First: *I'll find another place.* Then: *Even if I do, I won't be able to afford it. Who's going to give me a room for forty dollars a month?* Maybe God will intervene . . . somehow.

The pastor and his wife let her stay for several more weeks while she looked for housing, both on foot in the neighborhood and by car farther afield. Nothing was affordable. But one day when she set out walking from the house, she had only passed two driveways when she heard a voice. You might say an angel appeared, in the form of a neighbor.

"Honey, you look troubled. Come over here and tell me what's wrong."

JoeAnn looked over to see a kind-faced woman standing on

her front porch. She walked over to explain her dilemma.

Hearing JoeAnn's predicament, the lady nodded, said, "Come with me," and led JoeAnn into her house and up to the second floor. The woman's entire upstairs was a handsomely furnished apartment! "I'll set the rent the same as you've been paying, and you can move in tomorrow."

God's hand seemed to be moving all over JoeAnn's life. Not only did she find a wonderful place to live, her new landlady became her mentor, and under her guidance JoeAnn was able to grow that Sunday school to forty-five children and adults. She was drawn to deep faith, blind faith. She read books written by devout Christians through the ages. She found resonance in the words of Carmelite monk Brother Lawrence, who wrote: "Men invent means and methods of coming at God's love . . . and it seems like a world of trouble to bring oneself into the consciousness of God's presence. . . . Is it not quicker and easier just to do our common business wholly for the love of him?"

As with Brother Lawrence, the rise of faith in spirit called Joe-Ann to channel her conviction into practical application. Mulling over the neighborhood's lack of response when she tried to force-feed Sunday school to them, her understanding deepened. "I wanted to offer them Christ," she wrote in her journal. "Inside, I was singing the song, 'I offer Christ to you.' But the people said: 'We are not wanting Christ right now because we have our own set of burdens and circumstances.' I was trying to engage people about the gospel, but they said, 'We don't have shoes, we don't have food.'"

Heading to Sunday school one morning in her car, JoeAnn watched three church buses roll past a well-dressed lady who was walking along the sidewalk, carrying a gas can. *What does it mean to do the work of the Lord?* she said to herself, pulling over to help the lady. From that moment on, JoeAnn determined that being Christian begins with asking, "How can I help you?" It begins with assisting a person in need and not by having a predetermined agenda. She knew that the root of her ministry would begin with communing with God. Then she would use patience, insight, and relentless hard work to expand her fellowship.

While she devoted herself more to ministry, at the same time there lived in JoeAnn's heart one secret desire: she wanted a good husband. Every time she thought about having a husband, she just gave it to God. In the back of her Bible she made a list of characteristics she hoped God would provide in her mate: clean of drugs, alcohol, and tobacco; tall and handsome; a man of faith; a good provider; a man who loves children; and someone who won't waste his money on frivolities. At the Nazarene Bible Institute, she had turned away potential suitors who weren't on time for a date or dressed sloppy or, at the other end of the spectrum, wasted money on fancy clothes. "However he acts now is how he's gonna act when we're married, and I don't want any part of that," she'd tell her roommate.

Men may not know what women want, but other women do. One day when JoeAnn visited a sick lady in her home, the woman said, "Honey, get my purse." Rummaging around in the big bag, the woman smiled. "I got something for you," she said, and produced a small piece of paper with a handwritten message: *Monroe Ballard, Holiness Church.*

Monroe was the Sunday-school superintendent at Church of Christ Holiness U.S.A. and a Mississippi man who had grown up a few hours northwest of JoeAnn's home in Lucedale. Like Joe-Ann, Monroe was raised in the bosom of a farming family that thrived on hard work and family values. Unlike JoeAnn, Monroe enjoyed a childhood centered on his biological parents, Seth and Lucille Ballard. Monroe was born May 4, 1938, in Pocahontas, Mississippi. He seemed ready for this world, eager to take it on, hungry to see how it all worked. "Monroe never did learn to walk," his mother would say. "He just stood up one day, walked a few steps, and started running."

By the time he was ten, he was a woodsman, working four-hour stretches carrying timber from the forest and stacking it by the house. He thrived on the attention his parents gave him for working hard, and he looked for more chores. When his older brother and sister left home, he learned to hitch the mule, cut firewood with a handsaw, and plow fields. In the early years, although the Ballards had land, they did not know how to plant and garden, so the menu was particularly meager. On Mondays, his mother served onion gravy and cornbread; on Tuesdays, tomato gravy and cornbread; on Wednesdays, plain gravy and cornbread; on Thursdays, tomato gravy and cornbread; and on Fridays, syrup and cornbread.

She soon kept a prolific garden, however. Despite a limited number of staples to work with, she loved to cook and managed to fashion a tasty menu despite the meager food budget.

Monroe's father had taught him that herbs were medicine. They could be collected from the fields and forests and sold to help buy what they couldn't grow on the farm. Monroe could make medicinal teas and tinctures from what they gathered: sassafras for arthritis and gout, stinging nettle for internal bleeding, goldenrod for asthma and diabetes, cherry bark for coughs.

As the third oldest of eight children, Monroe learned by watching his parents how to be a master of frugality. He also learned how to take things apart and fix them. There was always a way to repair whatever was broken. Not everything could be made good as new, but most everything could be made good to go. When electricity was eventually installed in the house, he got the idea to make an electric fan to help them cool off in the Mississippi summer heat. "I made the fan too heavy to run," he wrote in his journals, "and a blade flew off and went for about one-eighth of a mile. I could have been cut to death by one disconnected metal blade." But as with other things, he didn't give up and would try again until he achieved his goal.

The Ballards owned their own home and land. When the family home burned down from a fire accidentally started by one of the kids, the Ballards moved into an abandoned schoolhouse with no plumbing. Like JoeAnn's parents, Monroe's parents never complained but instead kept cheerful hearts. Seth taught his son that everything he did was for the family, and family was all that mattered. "Son, remember this," he would say. "Do right, go straight, and take care of your home and family." Whenever Monroe took an odd job and earned money, he could hardly wait to share it with his parents. Monroe carried this joy of serving others with him, and anybody who knew him heard him repeat and live out his father's motto: "Do right, go straight."

As a boy he had trouble reading and was whipped at Springhill Consolidated School for this difficulty. At the time in the South, a whipping in school was accepted as a way of helping a child remember to do better next time. While Monroe struggled with reading, he worked hard in everything and excelled in many other ways.

After he began attending Mississippi's Piney Woods School, he was nicknamed "Time" because he was as punctual as a timepiece. Piney Woods was one of the few traditionally African American boarding schools in the nation. In his junior year, Monroe joined the Army Reserve, remained active through high school, and signed up for six months' active duty, which helped pay his way through junior college. He completed his bachelor's degree at his father's alma mater, Alcorn State University in Mississippi, the first land-grant college for black Americans.

Monroe was hired to teach sixth grade at Douglass Elementary School in Memphis and earned $350 a month—the most he had ever been paid in his life. Minimum wage in 1960 was one dollar an hour, and the average teacher's salary nationwide was around $400 per month. Besides being gainfully employed, Christian, and handy, Monroe was tall and strong and family-centered. On any woman's list, he would have been: check, check, check, check, and check.

When he greeted JoeAnn for the first time as she visited church that day, Monroe had given up on his own search for a spouse. He had very little experience dating and had decided to simply be faithful to the needs of the church. But something about Joe-Ann struck his heart. Despite his shyness (he often tried to hide behind sunglasses), he was drawn to her and made a point to chat casually with her after church.

Initially, JoeAnn was turned off by the dark glasses, wondering, "Who does he think he is, Ray Charles?" Yet something in Monroe's face was inviting. There was a great gentleness and patience about him.

They began to find opportunities to spend time together. If JoeAnn finished teaching Nazarene Sunday school in time to get to Monroe's church, she would be there. Soon Monroe asked her not on a date but to a church program. He asked her to join him for Vacation Bible School that summer.

"It was a grand opportunity to see how well we would work together on a given task," he wrote in his memoirs. Then, and only then, did he ask her out for dinner, and she accepted. Spending more time together, they developed a deep friendship. "As time passed, we grew closer," he wrote. "I began to talk about her when I went home to see my parents. My family thought it was very strange for me to find a mate, because I did not date around like most men."

By this time Monroe was taking some of his school kids for hikes and enrichment outings. He invited JoeAnn to come with them, and their compatibility grew along with their devotion to helping children in the community.

They had only been dating a few months when Monroe talked about marriage. "We know how to work together," he told her. "That's important for a husband and wife."

Deciding to marry Monroe was a big step for JoeAnn, especially since at the age of twenty-one, she had never been in a serious relationship with a man. But the two of them had a good feeling about their possibilities together. They believed that their union would be a big love, one that God would spread much far-ther than the four walls of their own home.

In order to buy a wedding dress and shoes, JoeAnn took on part-time work at the Blue Goose plant, which made men's work pants. (One black woman had applied for a sewing position at the plant before the Civil Rights Act passed and was denied, saying that black women were only hired to press fabric and pants.)

Thanksgiving Day 1966 found them in Lucedale, surrounded by dozens of family members from the Benjamin, Marshall, Law-rence, and Ballard tribes. "Twelve Lawrences settled on this land almost two hundred years ago," an elderly aunt said, launching into the story that was told every year around the Thanksgiving meal. She spoke slowly, weighing each word before releasing it into the hearts and minds of the family gathered 'round. "Back then there was no such thing as George County. George County was carved out of parts of Jackson and Green Counties. The Law-rence family dedicated part of this land for camp meetings; you know, that's the very place we still meet every fall for camp meet-ing. Folk came from Moss Point, Lucedale, Benndale, Pascagoula, Biloxi—all over, all coming to the tabernacle." When one of the teenagers at the table gave her a quizzical look, she said, "Baby, that's what we called the tent: the tabernacle."

There was much to be thankful for: the warmth of family, the abundance of homemade dishes on the table—and especially Joe-Ann and Monroe's wedding planned for the following day. Joe-Ann was blessed with so many relatives in George County that she simply invited the whole town of Lucedale and many of the folks in surrounding towns as well. Traditionally, weddings in Lu-cedale were held in a relative's house or the family's old home-stead; church weddings were for white folks and black folks who had a lot of money. But JoeAnn wanted a church wedding, and a church wedding is what she would have.

On November 25, 1966, the heralded day of JoeAnn and Mon-roe's wedding, people came from every corner of George County and arrived by every means possible: walking, riding horses or mules, driving in cars, and steering farm wagons. All in all, including Monroe's relatives, nearly four hundred people crammed into Mt. Pleasant United Methodist Church and spilled out onto the grounds. JoeAnn wore a long white dress and a veil of lace, both handmade by Ora Mae—for less than nine dollars.

Mt. Pleasant United Methodist Church had been founded by JoeAnn's great-great-grandparents, and it seemed that generations of relatives were present in spirit that day. Administering their vows was Rev. Warren Rogers, the pastor who had assigned JoeAnn to Memphis—an assignment that had led her to Monroe. JoeAnn and Monroe faced each other in the small wooden church packed with relatives; many more stood outside under pine trees that swayed in the slight breeze. They vowed to love and honor until death parted them; JoeAnn pledged to submit to her husband "even as the church submits to Christ, forsaking all others to cling to him with a love which fails not as long as you both shall live."

After an evening of prayers and blessings, food and fellowship, Monroe's brothers, Samuel and Sylvester, drove the newlyweds to the Sun-N-Sand Motor Hotel in Jackson, Mississippi. It was one of the few regional hotels that allowed black guests. (All across the country, black entertainers such as Lena Horne, Sammy Davis, Jr., Nat King Cole drew thousands of people to America's casinos, hotels, and bars—but as black people, they were not welcome as guests. It would be several more years before black people could drive up to the hotel of their choice and expect to get a room.) The Sun-N-Sand stood a few blocks from the state capitol in Jackson, its oversized sign and small dining room sporting a zesty orange-and-turquoise color scheme. It was the first time either of the newlyweds had stayed in a hotel. JoeAnn had brought sheets and towels in case they weren't provided. The rooms did not have telephones, but the lobby offered a rotary-dial phone with free calls.

The next day they drove to Monroe's sister's house, where Daisy made a big fuss over them, serving them a huge meal in the afternoon. When they returned to Memphis, JoeAnn moved in with Monroe in a room he rented from the Ware family. It was only $20 a month and allowed them to begin saving money for a home.

The work that had summoned JoeAnn to Memphis—resurrecting the Memphis South Church of the Nazarene—was complete. Rev. Robert Hires had been hired as the minister and was attracting a flock from the impoverished community that JoeAnn had enlivened. At twenty-one, she had managed to garner and feed the bodies and souls of a neighborhood in need. It had surely been an odyssey of trial and error, but it had allowed her to pull more determination, more focus, more inspiration from inside herself than she even realized was present. And now, she was ready for more. But first there was a home and a new life to set up with Monroe. They faced the first chapter of their married life with hearts full of faith, hope, and love—and about fifty dollars in savings.

∾ FOUR ∾
Here Come the Children

ONROE AND JOEANN DIDN'T SET OUT TO
create a free, home-based parenting program, but that is
what happened. It was purely voluntary and achieved without any
support from the government or human-service agencies—and
unlike anything ever seen in Memphis. The young couple vowed
to never take money for keeping the children because they wanted
the children to know—and never doubt—that they acted purely
out of love. "Because money doesn't change people," Monroe said.
"Only love changes people."

Their compassionate ministry gathered strength imperceptibly,
the way barges inch their way down the Mississippi River duti-
fully hauling tons of cargo to their destinations. But before the
Ballards' ministry could expand, their perspective about the poor
had to change. JoeAnn describes it like this: "We, along with other Christians we knew, drew a hard line when it came to offering
compassion to the poor. It was understood that a good Christian
would help people in need—to a point. And only if they first accepted Jesus Christ as their Savior."

In the Christian community, compassionate ministries remained controversial across the country. They wanted to bring
souls to Christ, but the unspoken consensus among congregants
was, "We don't want to bring in all these people with all their
needs." As JoeAnn describes it, "We want to see people healed,
but we don't want to get our hands dirty." Many ministries started
in response to natural disasters in other countries, but such efforts
were reserved for far-away places, places American Christians
didn't have to see on a daily basis. They were not for America's poor.

A theology of affluence had emerged after World War II, as Thomas G. Nees points out in his book *Compassion Evangelism*. "Poverty was viewed as the consequence of laziness, if not ungodliness. Social Darwinism . . . won the day. There seemed to be no reason for anyone to be poor." But the Ballards found a fresh pair of eyes with which to view their neighbors living in generational poverty. And it happened in part because of their constant exposure to people in need.

Monroe taught school with the same enthusiasm and methodology he had formed as the big brother on the family farm in Pocahontas. He was confident and successful as a teacher, and he never, ever took a sick day.

Although his students responded well to him, it wasn't long before Monroe became troubled. He could readily see that his students at Douglass Elementary needed more than science instruction. Many of them were not getting their basic needs met. Some needed clothes, some needed a bath, some had little to eat other than what was offered at school—and Monroe suspected that some of them left school each day with nowhere to go.

"How can they concentrate when they're hungry and dirty?" he asked JoeAnn. "How can I pretend to teach them academics when I know their lives must be unstable?" And he was certain that many of the children had never experienced a home church, had never been part of a faith community.

Each night after coming home from her part-time job as a cashier at the Sears department store in North Memphis, JoeAnn listened to her husband as he talked about the children he could not ignore. It was the moment the young couple had felt was coming: a calling to step up and do more.

By July 1967, less than a year into their marriage, JoeAnn and Monroe had saved nearly $2,500 to put a down payment on a house. Even though they did not have proof of the extracurricular work they had done—house painting, cake sales, and such—they had developed a rapport with the loan officer at the bank. He graciously included their part-time jobs as part of their combined annual income.

They found a two-bedroom, one-bath brick home, with an attic, a basement and a garage out back, at 933 Barbara Street that cost $11,500. The location was perfect, less than three miles from Douglass Elementary School where Monroe taught. Signing the closing papers at Leader Federal Savings & Loan in Memphis was the beginning of a ministry that would ultimately nurture thousands of young people in Memphis for many years to come.

The night they moved in, sitting in her new home looking at the mortgage papers, JoeAnn was struck by the distinctive script of the closing attorney, Ernest Bland Williams III. His handwriting was the most beautiful, the most perfect penmanship Joe-Ann had ever seen. Six years later she would see that handwriting again—and have good reason to remember it.

Their mission began with a single child.

Laura was nine years old and painfully thin when she arrived at the Ballards'. Her clothes were raggedy, but she was a spirited and obedient child. Although the referral had come through a local pastor, the Ballards felt strongly about involving the girl's mother in their ministry to Laura. They asked Laura's mother if the girl could come to their house for Sunday lunch, and she agreed without hesitation: the woman had eight other mouths to feed. It wasn't long before Laura became their first weekend daughter.

It seemed natural to sit at the dinner table as a family that Friday evening and say grace over JoeAnn's homemade meal. Afterward dinner Monroe tutored Laura while JoeAnn did the dishes. Then JoeAnn made sure the girl had a proper bath and put her to bed with a smile and a kiss, telling her, "Tomorrow we'll take you shopping, honey, and get you a pretty dress." On the sale rack in the back of Sears, JoeAnn found the perfect blue dress for Laura.

That afternoon, a slight wind kicked up, and Monroe showed Laura how to make a kite. It was a time-honored tradition for many country people; Monroe's brother Sam had passed the knowledge on to him. Monroe fashioned the frame from wooden dowels, notched them so he could attach spars, bound it together with string, and covered the frame with a large plastic bag. He tore a clean white rag into strips and tied them together to make the tail. Then they flew the kite together on the school grounds nearby.

Sunday morning at church, Laura was radiant in her new blue dress. As a regular weekend guest of the Ballards, Laura was like a flowering plant long denied water and sun. Once she got the care she needed, she began to bloom.

The Ballards took notice of compassionate acts offered by people with precious little to give. One of their early role models was Reverend Bass, a one-legged pastor who, through the years, would bring unkempt children with him to church. Most had been born to young girls who had had sex too soon, gotten pregnant, had no job skills, got on welfare, and then, in the absence of a better role model, spent their government checks on booze and partying. It was a problem that burned in North Memphis, just like the asphalt streets in July.

One day as church let out and congregants gathered on the sidewalk, Reverend Bass asked JoeAnn to meet him at a low-rent apartment complex where he lived. She knew the area, and had a feeling that she was about to be disgusted by the filth and stench of both the people and the garbage-ridden buildings. She was correct. Reverend Bass introduced her to two young sisters. The girls' clothes were grimy, but there was a brightness of spirit on their unwashed faces. Against all odds, a flame of hope lived inside them.

As the girls walked away, Reverend Bass popped the question: "Can you take them home next weekend and clean them up for church?"

"I'll have to discuss it with my husband," JoeAnn said. She could guess what Monroe would probably say, but it was important to have the discussion together before making a decision.

"No way to clean themselves up?" Monroe shook his head, his heart filled with compassion for them, as JoeAnn described their situation when she got home.

"When I was a boy on the farm, I had the same problem. All six of us kids slept in the same bed, and sometimes when we woke up, one of us had peed in the night. I would dress without bathing and put on the same unwashed clothes from the previous day. I must have smelled really bad to the other schoolchildren."

As superintendent of Sunday school for the Church of Holiness USA and director of religious education for adults and children, Monroe was a church leader. JoeAnn was a member and supporter. They hoped their work with the poor little girls would be met with approval, but they weren't certain that would happen. They knew people had covered their noses and whispered to one another when the Reverend had previously brought homeless or neglected children to church.

"My father taught me to watch out for the kind of gesture that could have an impact on a life," Monroe said, "and this looks like one of those chances."

Together, the young couple agreed to help the girls. And for the rest of their lives they would step toward suffering rather than away from it.

They gave the sisters a magical weekend at their home—which by the standards of many wasn't special at all. For numerous Americans, a warm bath, a balanced meal, and clean clothes are assured and taken for granted. But for those without access to such simple necessities, these things are so completely out of reach that they might as well be the stuff of royalty.

Sunday morning, JoeAnn styled the girls' freshly shampooed hair so that every strand lay perfectly platted and in place. She then clothed them in clean dresses, and they headed off to church. When the last notes of the organ player's hymn echoed in the room, and folks rose to greet one another, women flocked around Monroe and JoeAnn and the two girls. Their voices chimed in excited tones, welcoming the new children to their church.

"My, my! What beautiful girls!"

"What's your name, honey?"

"Aren't you a precious child!"

Something important and almost unnamable occurred in that moment, compelling JoeAnn to say, "These two sisters are the same girls you all complained about last week and the week before." JoeAnn felt herself taking a quiet yet public stand. It came from a level so deep inside her that she didn't need to explain it at all. She was standing up for those who couldn't speak for themselves. As she and Monroe had predicted, their gesture began to change their lives. It was apparent that children who needed help did not feel welcome at the Ballards' present church—and the Ballards no longer felt comfortable worshipping alongside people who could not be kind to children in need.

"These children need love, they need compassion. They don't need anybody else to judge and condemn them," JoeAnn said.

This realization led Monroe and JoeAnn to transfer their membership to the Friendship Church of the Nazarene on North Parkway. From that moment forward, the Ballards found room in their hearts and room in their modest home for children who needed what they had to offer. In church every Sunday and during the week at Douglass Elementary School, Monroe kept his eye out for children who seemed lost. He understood that they needed someone to look up to, someone to teach them the things that a good father would impart.

Monroe and JoeAnn began taking these children with them on weekend drives, weekend hikes in the country, and park outings. He would pile some of them in his new Ford Falcon while JoeAnn would fill her Oldsmobile with others. They'd give the kids one admonition: "Stay low, now, and be quiet so we don't attract attention."

It wasn't an issue of seat belts because seat belts wouldn't be required in Tennessee for another eighteen years.

But a carload of black faces attracted unwanted attention in the South at the time. It was understood in the '60s that antebellum etiquette remained the social norm; black people were to act subservient to whites at all times. They knew better than to try to enter "whites-only" restaurants, they understood they were not welcome to try on new clothes or hats in many stores, and they knew better than to congregate in cars or on the street or anywhere else. Keeping track of nine or ten kids in two cars was chaotic, but JoeAnn and Monroe operated with a deep conviction that they were involved in something much bigger than the few hours they spent with the children.

Their outings always consisted of driving somewhere, since the kids had no home life to speak of—plus the Ballards' tiny one-room apartment was hardly large enough to contain so many. The newlyweds began to dream out loud that if they only had a house, they could take in some of these children. It would not be the kind of place that most people imagined when they heard the words "foster home." JoeAnn and Monroe envisioned the kind of home that every child deserves, where food and clothes, love and discipline are given for free.

"I had often wondered: what has God put in me that I can use to help someone else?" JoeAnn says. "When we began offering ourselves to young people in need, my question was answered. There was something in me that knew how to be good to these kids."

But their dream suffered a major setback from the get-go. "I'm sorry," the loan officer told Monroe, "you don't qualify for a home mortgage."

Monroe was frustrated and disappointed, but he never became bitter that because he was a black man, his monthly salary was $50 less than what white teachers averaged for the same job. While that may not seem like much now, at the time, an extra $25 a month could make the difference between qualifying for a home mortgage or not.

70

Ever-resourceful, he found part-time work using his able hands and strong back. He painted houses. He hauled out his chain saw and ax and cut down trees for homeowners, often splitting the timber afterward for firewood. Every summer when the new Southern Bell telephone book came out, he worked part-time delivering them to homes and businesses. He also took a nighttime job at an automobile tire warehouse. After working all day teaching, he sorted and stacked tires for four hours before heading to their apartment to sleep, completely exhausted.

JoeAnn found a night job, cleaning the First Church of Nazarene. She also became a powerhouse of home industry, baking cakes for birthdays and special occasions, braiding rags together to make rugs, and taking on sewing just as her mother had. When someone gave JoeAnn a camera, she immediately set about photographing nature, pets, and people and selling the photos. Together, she and Monroe put an extreme focus on thriftiness and saved money like misers.

In 1968 when Dr. Martin Luther King Jr. came to Memphis, JoeAnn was nine months pregnant with her first child. Putting the last stitches in a baby bonnet for her first-born, she remembered hearing Dr. King for the first time back in 1963. That was the summer she had moved to New York City to live with her godmother and worked in a garment factory.

That summer King's speech from the steps of the Lincoln Memorial in Washington, D.C., electrified television and radio listeners worldwide. Fearlessly, King stood at the feet of Abraham Lincoln's larger-than-life seated statue and articulated the pain and disparity that black people felt in their bones. He described in no uncertain terms the "vast ocean of material prosperity" in the United States. With sizzling conviction he declared that "now is the time to make real the promises of democracy, to make justice a reality for all of God's children."

King's unwavering message of racial injustice in America incited many local whites across the country, some of whom feared that blacks would riot, others who feared that blacks would work harder for equality. When black students attempted to enroll in the University of Alabama, Gov. George Wallace called for armed Alabama National Guardsmen to stop them. In a June 1963 address to the nation, President John F. Kennedy reminded the country that "when Americans are sent to Vietnam or West Berlin, we do not ask for whites only." Five months later Kennedy was assassinated while riding in a motorcade, greeting the people of Dallas, Texas. Vice President Lyndon B. Johnson, who had worked on the Civil Rights Act of 1957, became the thirty-sixth president of the United States. It was a dark time in American history.

The occasion of King's April 1968 visit to Memphis was the sanitation workers' strike. The final blow triggering the strike of fourteen hundred black workers was the death of two workers. When they were crushed to death in the garbage grinder, it was seen to be an easily preventable tragedy. Certain city officials were known to be members of the Ku Klux Klan. The city of Memphis was poised for a battle of wills, and the fight had been a long time coming.

King aroused Memphis's downtrodden workers with a grace and power that was utterly unique to him, calling their working conditions "a crime." On the day before a scheduled second strike, April 3, Dr. King delivered a spellbinding fifteen-minute public speech in which he invoked images of the Promised Land and called for courage, steadfastness, and nonviolence in response to fear. People were so aroused that city leaders called for a dawn-to-dusk curfew. At 5:56 p.m., the road-weary Nobel Prize laureate walked from his room in the Lorraine Motel onto the balcony and was gunned down.

A torn country watched the television news with horror that evening. CBS news anchor Walter Cronkite called King "an apostle of nonviolence in the civil rights movement."

For black Americans, it was a hopeless day and one that triggered furious emotions. In Memphis, where a teenager had been killed the week before in violence following the sanitation strike, angry black men took to the streets, smashing windows and looting. President Lyndon B. Johnson called for nonviolence as the governor of Tennessee activated four thousand National Guardsmen to the streets of Memphis.

Across Memphis, armed National Guardsmen stopped pedestrians and drivers, particularly black citizens, turning them back if they couldn't prove their travel was absolutely necessary. With the streets under armed guard, JoeAnn's doctor took precautionary measures. He admitted her to the hospital several days before her due date and advised Monroe to go to work each day as usual, stopping by the hospital on the way home. The rooms in Collins Chapel Hospital offered neither televisions nor telephones, leaving JoeAnn in a news blackout for several days before she gave birth.

Because of the National Guardsmen patrolling the streets, Monroe was unable to be present when Ephie Jean was born April 10, 1968. But in a photograph taken soon after her birth, his huge hands gently hold baby Ephie, his face bearing the expression of a man whose heart has been utterly rendered.

The injustice of not being able to walk or drive freely could have infuriated the couple, but JoeAnn had a different read on it. "I never thought of being angry," she said. "I'm not afraid of being vocal when necessary. But I have always been a person who spent my time looking at how to make things better for the future rather than letting present circumstances stop me from being an agent of change. When Ephie was born, my thought was, 'How can I make Memphis a better place for the next baby to be born?' Like the Bible says, there is a secret to being content in every situation, whether well fed or hungry, whether living in plenty or in want."

73

✆ FIVE ✆
ℒiving in ℭreative ℭhaos

A CLOSE FRIEND, ROGER McGEE SR., HELPED Monroe with renovations on the Ballards' new home; they enlarged the kitchen, added a den, and created two more bedrooms out of the existing square footage. When the last brushstroke of paint was dry on the new bedrooms, Monroe and JoeAnn welcomed in more weekend children. Over time, hundreds of young people passed through the door of the Ballards' home. Since none of the children was sent from an agency, "foster care" doesn't adequately define what the Ballards offered, but the federal Social Services Information System has invented a name for such situations: Family Preservation Services.

Federal entitlements recognize that at-risk children may need time to be "absent" from their current living environment, whether they live with a blood relative or a state-certified foster family. The idea is that by giving respite to the person or people responsible for full-time care of the child, the home environment might improve—or at least not deteriorate any further. Family preservation care can prevent Social Services from needing to step in and remove a child from his or her home, causing added disruption to the child and the whole family system.

Perhaps most importantly, the care offered by the Ballards sent a targeted message to children and their families that they didn't need to do anything at all to "qualify" for help, that they deserved a stable home, and that they were worthy of love.

As for the parents of the children, it isn't important to chronicle how they fell short. Some were unemployed. Some had grown up in generational poverty. Some wanted their children to finish high school but didn't have the means to help them at home. Some were high-school dropouts who resented their children's attendance in school. Some suffered from drug abuse, sexual abuse, physical abuse. Some loving parents had fallen on hard times and just needed help getting through their compounded challenges.

The common denominator in those first families the Ballards helped was that they were trapped below the poverty line with no visible way out. Their children, for the most part, did not know that life could include sitting with family and friends around a table overflowing with healthy food—something the average American takes for granted. As one news article about the Ballards' work explained, "Most of the children . . . feel more at home in the Ballards' home than in their own home."

The relationship between the Ballards as surrogate parents and the parents or legal guardians of the children was characterized by trust and open communication. JoeAnn and Monroe regularly phoned parents to discuss what was going on with the kids and to plan best-case scenarios for their immediate reality and long-term futures. All visits between them were planned and agreed on in advance. For those young women who did not come out of foster homes but needed to be out of their environments for a time because of difficult circumstances, JoeAnn was careful to invite the biological mothers into her home so they could observe how she ran a household and in general kept the children clothed, fed, and disciplined. Most often the mother's primary problem was that she never had a proper role model to follow but instead had a life filled with people who were hardened and self-centered. In these situations the Ballards' goal was always to assist in reconciliation between parents and their children.

The first weekend visitor in their new home was Elizabeth, one of Monroe's sixth-grade students whom Monroe and JoeAnn had already taken on several day outings. She relished their attention, and her mother instantly consented to weekend stays. Like most of the Ballards' relationships with their kids, it was a long-term commitment. Elizabeth was the Ballards' weekend daughter from sixth grade, in 1967, until she graduated from high school. With their encouragement and support, Elizabeth later moved to Florida to attend college and found work in social services. The home Monroe and JoeAnn gave her Friday through Sunday was, in the end, the most enriching family experience of her short life. Sadly, when Elizabeth was in her thirties, she was diagnosed with cancer and died soon after.

The Ballards had only been married for two years when Monroe's brother Sam came to live with them for a time. By then four girls were living with them occasionally as well as a woman with three children who needed temporary housing. Two of the girls arrived at the door one rainy day, clutching paper grocery bags stuffed with the few clothes they owned. The look in their eyes was indescribably vacant. Their older sister, who had cared for them single-handedly for years, stood behind them. The girls' father, a poor Mississippi farmer, had died young, leaving the family penniless; no one knew where their mother was. JoeAnn and Monroe welcomed the teenage girls into their home and saw them through high-school graduation. The whole Ballard clan showed up and cheered for the girls at their graduations, just as they did for all of their children.

The Ballards' approach to parenting was long on love and short on expectations. Although JoeAnn called the girls who lived full-time at their house "children," many of them were eighteen and older. While some of them had been raised by their biological parents, many had been raised in foster care where they had essentially been slaves, forced to work with no pay. Their foster parents made the girls raise the younger foster children and take care of other household responsibilities that were too demanding for them at such young ages.

These girls had never owned a doll, never played with a dog, never had real childhoods. Many had been taken in by a relative who insisted, "You gotta fend for yourself" or by foster parents who were only interested in receiving money from the government.

A refreshing change to these girls' bleak backgrounds, the Ballards' vision—born out of their own loving childhoods—was to give unconditionally, without soliciting any kind of payback: the act of giving was their only reward. As a wise man once said, "A gift is a completed transaction."

The only expectations placed on anyone who lived in the Ballard home were those that encouraged responsibility and maturity. While the girls had specific chores, the Ballards refused to use the older children to babysit the younger ones. The kids contributed to the household by cooking one meal a week. If they didn't know what to do in a kitchen, JoeAnn taught them basic cooking skills. Their second responsibility was to stay in school, and the Ballards made sure the girls had help at home with schoolwork. Third, the kids knew that the Ballards envisioned them going to college and eventually owning their own homes, and they were to adopt this mindset for themselves. In an environment of love and trust, the young people who moved into the Ballard home earned their high-school diplomas—often becoming the first in their families to do so. They worked hard and saved their money, leaving the Ballard home when they went off to college, got married, or could move into their own homes. Fourth, they were expected to save money in order to accomplish all the things envisioned for them.

To help the kids learn to save money, JoeAnn taught them the same method her father had taught her. "When I was eight, my brother ten, and my sister twelve," she recalls, "we wanted to go out and pick cotton and peas in the white folks' fields with everyone else. We had our own farm, but it didn't take long to harvest it. My dad agreed it was a good idea for us to also work in other fields, so he had my mother get us three half-pint fruit jars and put our names on them." Every afternoon when they got home from picking cotton, JoeAnn and her siblings would put money their money in their jars. "At that time, I didn't know how to count money, but I knew how to watch it and judge by how full the jar was," she says. "I would ask my dad if it was 'big' yet, and he would say that it was getting there. I'm sure he put money into my jar to make it as full as my older brother's and sister's." Before school started in the fall, their parents would buy their school clothes and book bags, allowing JoeAnn and her siblings to use the money they had earned to buy extra things they really wanted for school. Monroe and JoeAnn used this same simple but effective way of saving money with their own children and foster children.

Their idea of discipline involved constant support and guidance, what JoeAnn called environmental control.

"Discipline's not a one-shot deal," JoeAnn says. "It's more of a system. Our children understood from the beginning that they can't get away with bad behavior. Newcomers see the other children acting with respect, and they follow that model."

With good behavior as the norm, a child who chose to misbehave could not garner support from the others. When a child was caught acting out, a simple reprimand was usually all that was necessary. For most children in the South, getting a spanking from a parent or a teacher was a way of life, but spankings were seldom needed in the Ballard household.

Faced with an array of challenges from different children on a daily basis, Monroe and JoeAnn took on one problem at a time. They celebrated even the smallest improvements and successes. They never expected praise from others. They modeled generosity in a way that some people might not understand. If a child displayed selfishness, the Ballards responded with generosity. When a boy continually came to their door asking for money to take the bus to work, they knew he could afford a twenty-cent bus fare, but they gave him two dimes, anyway. Every time the boy asked, they gave him his bus fare, with the inner conviction that when he began earning regular paychecks, he would take care of his own transportation—and he did. When JoeAnn found apple cores and banana peels under the beds of two of their full-time girls, she didn't reprimand them. Instead, understanding their background and their resulting fear that they needed to hoard to have enough to eat, JoeAnn took a big bowl from the kitchen cabinet, filled it with fruit, and delivered it to the girls' room, saying, "You can have all the fruit you want; just put the peels and cores in the trash can."

One of the girls they took in had been brought up by a relative who was a prostitute and a drug addict. Rarely was there any food in her former home, and the young teenager had been told that if she wanted to eat, she had better use what she had to earn some money. The girl nonetheless got herself off to school each day, but the other kids ran from her because she smelled so bad, having no running water at home. Adding insult to injury, sometimes the teacher told the girl to stand by an open window so she wouldn't stink up the whole classroom.

She eventually became pregnant, and her relative died of an overdose. But she went to church, in hopes of somehow finding a better life. Seeing the pregnant teenager at church, Monroe and JoeAnn stepped in and began taking her for prenatal check-ups at their doctor and feeding her. They soon took the girl into their home, made sure she had what she needed for the baby, and helped her go to college.

As JoeAnn points out, sex for survival is common in the inner city.

"Leaving inner-city young people with no one to guide them is like leaving a time bomb to explode." She and Monroe dealt with sexual promiscuity from the Christian standpoint that premarital sex is wrong. As the numbers of children born out of wedlock increased along with the divorce rate, JoeAnn and Monroe found simple, profound ways to teach the benefits of sexual purity and marriage. They invited groups of children and parents for dinner and showed them a home video of their wedding in the small church in Lucedale. It wasn't a fancy movie—in fact, there was no sound—but it made the perfect backdrop for JoeAnn and Monroe to tell stories of the rewarding experience of having a wedding and sharing that day with friends and family.

Word spread quickly about the Ballards.

Like the legendary Pied Piper, Monroe and JoeAnn found children magnetizing toward them. Monroe prepared additional rooms, and they took in more girls from Friday through Sunday. Soon JoeAnn and Monroe had ten young girls on the weekends, sometimes a few more or a few less. With a house full of girls spending every weekend in their home, Monroe and JoeAnn didn't feel equipped to take boys into their home, but they soon felt compelled to find other ways to help the young men in their sphere of influence.

For the young men who came their way, Monroe took them under his wing, offering them fatherly love and useful skills. Eric followed in Monroe's footsteps as a handyman who could build or fix just about anything; Marvin learned to barbeque chicken on the backyard grill, and all of the boys learned basic home re-pairs under Monroe's careful eye. As a family project, they built a homemade merry-go-round for the backyard. However, even as he taught them skills, Monroe always encouraged the young people he mentored to get an education.

In the 1950s there was a big push in the African American community for young people to go to college. At some point, though, it became the acceptable standard to simply obtain a trade. As a result, a generation of black young adults had trades but no business sense. JoeAnn says, "We should have been say-ing that while it's OK to get a trade, you must also go to college. Monroe and I told our children that it was fine if they decided to become automobile mechanics, but they must first go to four years of college. We wanted them to be prepared to own the shop if they ever felt the desire to do so." In the back of his mind, Monroe was always dreaming of a way to help more kids go to college.

With each new child, there were surprises. Arthur, an eight-year-old, managed to overcome his excruciating shyness one day after church to ask JoeAnn if he could come to dinner. The nine other children at the table were initially too busy eating and talking to notice Arthur scooping mashed potatoes and gravy with his fingertips, but his hosts looked on with compassion, shocked to realize that no one had ever shown the child how to use a fork, spoon, or knife. As the meal progressed, no one who noticed the boy's crude eating habits judged him, no one made fun of him, no one said a word about it. But after the meal, Monroe sat down beside Arthur, pointed to the utensils and said, "Son, I'm going to show you how to use these." It took many Sundays of patient teaching to undo eight years of finger eating, and along the way Monroe learned that the child had rarely seen cooked food; instead, he had eaten bread, snacks, and finger foods most of his life. Monroe kept at his task and maintained complete confidence in the boy until he had learned proper table manners. Arthur later graduated from high school, moved west, and found work. Like some of the other children the Ballards helped, Arthur had suffered from malnutrition during his infancy and formative years, and as an unfortunate result, died young.

There were so many children like Arthur, who were hungry and desperate for a square meal and for love. One day Monroe parked behind a store and left JoeAnn waiting in the car while he went inside. Hearing noise coming from a nearby dumpster, she watched to see what was going on. Before long, the heads and hands of two adolescent boys popped up. The boys climbed from the dumpster as JoeAnn got out of her Buick—which had replaced her treasured Oldsmobile—and approached them. "All right, now," she said, "what are you fine little boys doing in that dumpster?"

One clutched a McDonald's bag in his hand; the other had a half-eaten box of donuts. "We come here every day," the taller one said.

"What for?" she asked, knowing the answer but not wanting to believe it.

"For food, lady."

JoeAnn felt her heart warm as she looked at the innocent faces of those hungry little boys standing in a Memphis, Tennessee, alleyway and eating from a dumpster. She smiled. "Maybe you can come to my house one day and eat with my family." Some people—probably most of us—would have said a prayer for the boys, maybe given them some coins, and left it at that with a shake of the head. But JoeAnn found out where the boys lived, went to their mother, and was granted permission to feed them, take them shopping, and bring them to church with her.

The Ballards' typical child had not eaten breakfast and wasn't sure where the next meal—or any meal—would come from. But Sunday dinner at JoeAnn and Monroe's house was a feast of homemade cooking. They ate corn on the cob, sweet potatoes, and JoeAnn's fried chicken. If they couldn't scrounge together enough chairs for all of the children who showed up for dinner, Monroe insisted on eating standing up, beaming with delight throughout the meal. After dinner JoeAnn made sure everyone had a paper bag filled with leftovers to take home with them.

Over time, about twenty young people of all ages came to the Ballard home every Sunday for dinner—hungry not just for the food but also for the compassion turned their way. Making ends meet called for creativity, especially for JoeAnn, who wanted to feed every hungry mouth. Having grown up in a rural community where nearly everyone in town was a relative, JoeAnn approached the proprietors of stores she frequented, asking if they had anything they could contribute to help feed the hungry. She quickly found hearts willing to share what extra bounty they had. She became a master of conservation, doing whatever it took to gather enough food and clothes for the kids who came to her home. Driving around the back of a grocery store, she saw the produce man with a mound of fresh heads of cabbage, stripping off the darkened, dirty or bruised outer leaves.

"Excuse me," she asked. "What are you going to do with those leaves?"

"They go to the hogs," the man said, glancing up and continuing to work.

"Can I have 'em?"

The produce man stopped what he was doing and looked past JoeAnn at the small heads barely visible in the back seat of her car. From that moment on, she could count on him to save fruits and vegetables that were about to go to the hogs.

Encouraged, she visited other grocery stores and asked them for help. JoeAnn saw firsthand the enormous level of waste in U.S. food resources. According to the National Resources Defense Council, 30 to 40 percent of the edible food in the United States is discarded each year. Enormous ongoing patterns of waste exist in the U.S. food supply chain, from farms to warehouses, from restaurant buffets to school cafeterias. Households too buy and store food that goes to waste each day. Grocery stores overstock fresh produce, make ready-to-eat food on a daily basis, and throw out all edibles that are damaged, expired, or have outdated promotional packaging. With necessity as the mother of invention, JoeAnn began to explore the gap and successfully tap the surplus in Memphis to feed her ever-growing family.

This was also a time when scouring the county dump for supplies was commonplace, at least among people with low incomes. Clothes, furniture, and appliances were routine finds, but JoeAnn's favorite discoveries were truckloads of brand new but imperfect manufactured goods. A company might dump an entire batch of toilet tissue or disposable diapers because they were the wrong color or had a seam in the wrong place. She frequented one landfill in Mississippi where a fabric manufacturer dumped large bolts of fine cloth with a pattern that had been misprinted. She found silk and chambray, corduroy and linen, then sewed the fabrics into housecoats, dresses, and shirts.

JoeAnn made it her business to find out what each child needed when he or she walked through the door; then she set about providing what was lacking, be it food, clothes, shoes, help with homework, an attentive ear, a kind word, or a moment of prayer. She knew she couldn't do it all herself but quickly found she had a knack for leading people and for organizing who would do what to ensure everyone got what was needed.

"That was our introduction to what we have always called foster care,'" JoeAnn says. "These were the moments that would define my life for years to come—combing hair, shopping for dresses at J.C. Penney's, buying the right groceries to make a perfect Sunday dinner. God used these seemingly small things to shape me into a person He could use. But the journey was long and tedious."

You could say the Ballard household was in a constant state of creative chaos, with so many people coming and going. Two permanent members were also added to the family. JoeAnn and Monroe's second daughter, Linda LaVonne, was born on a hot summer day, June 29, 1971 (first-born Ephie had just turned three). With impeccable timing, soon after Linda's birth, Ora Mae, the woman JoeAnn had always thought of as "Mama," came to live with them. Ora Mae's husband, DeLoach, had died in Lucedale in 1969, and Ora Mae was the kind of woman who was happier when needed. In a house full of foster children and assorted family members, Ora Mae was the perfect complement as she cooked, cleaned, tended to her grandbabies, and mothered everyone in the house.

A home video from the early 1970s depicts a house full of clean, well-dressed children of different ages relaxing, laughing, eating at a table with a sparkling-white tablecloth, and behaving like a typical family.

In one clip the children sit on the floor of the comfortable but crowded living room, carefully arranging pieces of broken dishes—which JoeAnn had received as a donation from a local store—like porcelain jigsaw puzzles, gluing them together to have more plates to accommodate everyone. JoeAnn's mother, Ora Mae, tries to hide from the camera; Monroe's brother Sylvester, who often joined the family on Sundays as well, is the image of composure as he sits with a child and conducts Bible study.

Monroe's head nearly touches the doorframe as he moves, smiling, from one room to the next. He wears a crisp button-down shirt and a tie. JoeAnn is working at the stove in one scene, and in another she is perched at a small metal table—her portable office—talking on the phone with a parent. Her "office" is just big enough for a small pile of paper, a telephone, and a manual type-writer.

The love, the house, and the grocery bill kept on growing. Taking in children on a schoolteacher's salary demanded making do and doing without, as JoeAnn and Monroe had both been raised. To supplement Monroe's monthly salary of $350, JoeAnn and Monroe continued to work side jobs every chance they got. Sometimes JoeAnn worked as a substitute teacher in one of the local schools, allowing them to catch up a little. Later, JoeAnn found part-time work as a teacher's aide at Douglass Elementary. Joe-Ann also had a knack for getting good prices for used cars, which is how she and Monroe had obtained the roomy old Buick that they drove for the next thirteen years and how she launched into another side business. On Saturdays while Ora Mae stayed home with the children, JoeAnn and Monroe scouted cars for friends and neighbors, driving down to the local dealership, choosing a car, and negotiating the price—for which JoeAnn received a fee for her time.

Monroe managed the finances. By all accounts, he was tight with money. Constantly documenting expenses in pocket-sized spiral notebooks, he made lists of every penny spent and noted what they needed to save for next. If they made a purchase, it was well planned and the money saved up in advance. One of the things they always saved for was an annual special meal out with their children. By the spring, they had saved enough to treat all the kids to a nice meal at an Italian restaurant. Eating out was not only a special enjoyment but also a teaching environment for proper eating habits and table manners. "Monroe and I would take twenty-five kids out to eat," JoeAnn laughs, telling the story years later. "It was the only time all year that I'd get to go to a restaurant. I dressed up like I was going to a country club. None of those kids had ever been to a restaurant in their entire lives. It would cost about $130, but we would put our money aside all year to make that happen."

Though they loved the path God had them on, both Monroe and JoeAnn felt the strain of trying to do so much at once. They were pulled in many directions, taking care of their own children as well as a handful of others every weekend plus jobs, church, and school activities. They spent the first twelve years of their marriage nurturing about three hundred children. While most of the kids they mentored and loved lived elsewhere, seventy-five girls spent at least one night with the Ballards in the first decade of their marriage. When one of their girls planned to marry, they did not wash their hands of her. To the contrary, they usually helped finance the wedding one way or another and then advised the couple as they worked toward homeownership. Their parenting never ended.

Nonstop surrogate parenting, working part-time outside the home, and round-the-clock donation work—solicitations and pick-ups, organization, storage, and delivery—took its toll on Joe-Ann's health. She was hospitalized twice with miscarriages. Money was always in short supply; it seemed that as soon as they had raised enough to help one child, two others needing financial assistance of some kind came into their lives.

Monroe was a powerful presence in the home, constantly sacrificing, helping all of the children with their homework before heading to the garage late at night to work on a side job, like making window bars for air conditioners for various clients. At six in the morning, he'd get up and ring the house buzzer he'd created and installed to wake the children. At seven he would head out the door to his students at Douglass. As one of the children would say later of Monroe, "He set the bar high, and then he jumped over it."

86

How did Monroe and JoeAnn manage to stay happily married while raising so many children amidst crushing financial and emotional tensions? It helped that JoeAnn and Monroe had each grown up in homes where their elders modeled strong marriages and wise parenting built on a godly foundation. JoeAnn and Monroe each possessed a high tolerance for the chaos that thrives in homes with many children. Each knew how to hold tight to a budget, so as JoeAnn says, "The lights were always on, and the mortgage was always paid—even though it looked sometimes like that would not happen." They weren't afraid of hard work. They had live-in help from JoeAnn's able-bodied, hard-working mother. They walked closely with God, which saw them through the challenge of each new dawn. Every morning Monroe and JoeAnn spent time reading the Bible and praying and also had a family devotion with the children each night. They held family conversations and guidance meetings with the kids once a week.

Another key to their successful marriage was the conscious decision to be a force of unity. Within their own home they were consistently, unfailingly unified as a couple and respectful of each other. As JoeAnn recalls, "We always had strong communication and agreement on what we were doing. The responsibilities we had as a young couple made us strong, and when there was tension, it was short lived because we had to move on to the business of running our home. We could not stand around and be mad all day. My husband valued my opinion and I, his. We tried never to cross a line that was offensive to the other, like draining the checkbook, running the car until the gas gauge was empty and not filling it up, leaving the house without telling someone where you were going, eating another person's food or drink without asking, discussing our personal business in public, speaking loudly to each other. We always kept a deep respect for each other. It was our way of life."

SIX
Outside Four Walls

IN THE BASIN COMMUNITY GIVING TO A NEIGHBOR was simply a way of life. If a person died and the family couldn't afford to bury him, the whole town took on the responsibility. When the roof on JoeAnn's parents' house had been damaged, neighbors showed up to help DeLoach repair it. And in the last days of his life, neighbors arrived at the doorstep every day to help him through his final transition.

Social-welfare programs were created in an odd juxtaposition to the free foster care that JoeAnn and Monroe were providing on an ever-expanding basis. Medicare had come on the scene in 1965 when Congress passed the Social Security Act, offering limited health insurance to people 65 and older, regardless of income or medical history. Medicaid provided basic health care for low-income Americans. One effect of social welfare was of particular significance for black Americans, who now found themselves waiting for medical care along with white patients—in formerly segregated facilities.

But the deeply harmful results of social-welfare programs have only been seen in hindsight. As the National Association of Black Social Workers points out, welfare "has failed to provide the resources necessary to gain a footing to move from welfare to adequate earning; it has penalized families that try to supplement income with earnings and work by too quickly decreasing public assistance; and it has employed policies that make public assistance to families dependent on the absence of a male in the house."

By the time the new millennium arrived, there had been de-

cades of erosion in poor black families who still continue to stag-
ger under the strain of low wages, unemployment, job dislocation,
lack of education, and lack of programs to motivate them to succeed.

Often JoeAnn served as an advocate for people trying to navi-
gate the maze of federal programs. One woman came to her when
her Social Security check had mysteriously stopped coming. First
JoeAnn created a power-of-attorney letter between her and the
woman, had it notarized, and sent it to the appropriate Social Security office. Then when JoeAnn called the office to get to the bottom of the problem, a flat voice answered, "We can't release that
information."

"But I sent you a notarized letter authorizing me to handle her
affairs."

"Those files are in another department."

"Is there someone else I can talk to about this?"

"No."

"May I speak to your supervisor?"

"He's not at this number: he's at another phone number."

"May I have that number?"

"I can't give that number out."

But the woman at the Social Security office underestimated
the obstinacy of the woman on the other end of the line to cut
through the absurdist maze. JoeAnn dialed that number over and
over again asking the same question until it became perfectly clear
that she wasn't giving up. She was transferred at last to the supervisor, who apologized, uncovered the problem, and restored the
woman's benefits.

Time—and change—marched on.

The euphoria of seeing American astronauts walking on the
moon faded as the U.S. stepped up its involvement in the Vietnam War, instituting a military draft to ensure an adequate supply of troops. The reality of America's poor came briefly into the
limelight when President Lyndon B. Johnson declared a "War on

Poverty" in 1964, and black nationalist Malcolm X was shot to death at a political rally in Harlem the same year. As the tumultuous years carried into the '70s, JoeAnn and Monroe's home was a peaceful place for all who sought refuge there. With so many mouths to feed and bodies to clothe and shelter, the needs became greater. In addition, as word got out in the community about the Ballards' unflagging generosity, more and more people sought them out for help, and their ministry began to stretch outside the walls of their home. Thankfully a supply of donors always seemed to show up right when they were needed. As the Ballards' reputation in Memphis spread, whenever someone had a surplus—food, candy, shoes, clothing, furniture, toys—they were called.

At eight o'clock each night, after the children went to bed, JoeAnn and Monroe left Ora Mae in charge and headed out in their red 1956 pickup truck, rounding up donated items. JoeAnn maintained two lists: one for items they had or were about to pick up and one for individuals who had contacted her for help. JoeAnn's goal was to give everything away within twenty-four hours. Whenever possible, she asked the recipients to be part of the hauling and delivering process.

One cold winter night a girl named Louise who frequently stayed with the Ballards on the weekends, came to their home wearing a man's bathrobe for an overcoat. When JoeAnn realized Louise didn't own a coat, she made it her mission to find one for her. The next week when she went to a local department store to pick up the surplus items the manager had begun to donate, she just knew she would find a coat. But there were plenty of clothes but no coat. Disappointed, she began to drive away, but the manager flagged her down, waving for her to stop. He said that during a recent fashion show, someone had spilled something on a coat, and he hadn't taken the time to clean it. JoeAnn recalls, "I pulled the coat out of the bag and saw the most beautiful coat I had ever seen. It was just Louise's size."

While most of the donations they received were very useful,

sometimes a gift could be a bit of a burden; but the Ballards never turned away anything. The year JoeAnn was pregnant with Linda, they were given seven hundred pounds of chocolate eggs. She carried them all back home in two car trips, trying to appreciate the gift while she also tried not to strain her muscles.

Trouble occasionally arose as they tried to distribute gifts in the neighborhood, and each time JoeAnn reassessed her methods. When she wanted to give basketballs to kids in a church youth program, she cleared it through the proper channels—but at the last minute someone called an impromptu phone meeting and reversed the permission. The Ballards only found out when they showed up for the big day. "We had gotten up early, packed the truck, collected balls and materials, and arrived at the church at 9:30 in the morning," JoeAnn says. "We planned to pass out fliers for the church while we played games and to give out some of the donated items we had collected. But at 9:45 the pastor came flying around the corner, waving us away and saying, 'You can't do this.' We began collecting all those things and putting them back in the truck. I was so upset, I was crying. Monroe was just cool daddy, not showing anything."

Considering the struggle of trying to work through a church, the Ballards decided to operate out of their own den. They turned their garage into storage that functioned as an independent clothing- and food-distribution center. When their garage was completely filled with donated goods, they borrowed space in the garages of their neighbor and Monroe's brother Sylvester as well as a storage building associated with their church. "Some people just stop by the house asking for a sweater or a pair of shoes," JoeAnn told a reporter at the time. "One little girl came by and found all the shoes she needed for her family, except for a pair for herself. So, we went out and bought a pair for her. We do that and enjoy it. We don't think of it as a burden."

By the time the Ballards held their first *Come One, Come All* Christmas party in 1973, they had seventeen steady supporters,

91

including individuals, businesses, and churches. JoeAnn was regularly on the phone calling local businesses for help, especially in early December as they prepared to buy Christmas presents for dozens of kids. They expected sixty children on December 22. The Ballards had a goal that is unusual by most American's standards: celebrate the birth of Christ with their kids and give them a present—but not focus on presents. On a shoestring budget, they wanted each child at the table to have a gift.

"My husband and I worked hard all year long to save money and to be sure we got one very special gift for each child—no strings attached," JoeAnn says. "We had one rule: they did not need to get us a gift. If they insisted on getting us something, it could not cost more than five dollars. When those kids got older, they turned into adults who said, 'We're going to help others just like you helped us.'"

The girls who were currently living with them full-time—Williestein, Ora, and Vera Ann—were pictured with JoeAnn and Monroe in a December 6, 1973, article in the *Memphis Press-Scimitar*, the afternoon paper. "Tuna salad may be the main course, instead of the hoped-for ham, turkey, or hen with trimmings," the article said. "The couple depends on their own resources and the generosity of others."

After the article appeared, checks began to come in the mail from well-wishers who wanted the Ballards to have enough money to buy presents and food for their Christmas party. The largest check, for one hundred dollars, was written in an elaborate script that JoeAnn recognized with a smile: Ernest Bland Williams III.

It was a very big Christmas dinner, *much* bigger than originally anticipated. "Two hundred and fifty people showed up at our house, and we were delighted to have them," Monroe wrote afterward. "Our entire house was filled with people, all of them happy and lively at the party." The Christmas parties became a time-honored tradition, still carried out to this day.

Rather than simply relying on donations from other people,

JoeAnn was always looking for ways to earn more money, and from 1969 to 1974 this included expanding outlets for her photography. Memphis was a playground for a photographer, with plenty of interesting faces and events. She was able to sell her photographs to publishing houses and magazines. She also made extra money photographing weddings. When video cameras became readily available and more affordable for consumers, she taught herself how to use one and got hired to videotape weddings for a small fee. In addition to bringing in more income, JoeAnn wanted to pass on her skills to the children in her sphere of influence. She combined a love of photography with her children's activities and started a camera club, contacting the Kodak Company for sponsorship. Sure enough, they sent her a camera and sufficient film for the club.

Soon the Ballard family grew once again. JoeAnn and Monroe's third child was born into a large, blended family of two siblings, JoeAnn's mother, and several full-time and weekend foster children. Born on March 15, 1976, Monroe Jr. weighed six and a half pounds despite being several weeks premature. Monroe lovingly called his son Baby Boy. They were delighted to have another child to raise up in love and to teach to serve others.

After staying home for a few years with the children and doing odd jobs here and there, JoeAnn took a job at a local department store. When she called to ask about a job, she was told there was an opening in the millenary department, but when she showed up, they told her the only job was in the kitchen. In those days of continuing racial tension, she knew why the only job offered to her was in the kitchen, but with their growing financial needs, she didn't bicker over where she worked.

"My first day on the job, the lady who hired me was astounded," remembers JoeAnn. "I came overdressed for the job to make a statement that I did not belong in the kitchen. I was always respectful, though, and did everything I was told—wash the dishes, mop the floors, bus the tables—while wearing high-heeled shoes."

This job turned out to be a blessing when one of the Ballards' foster daughters needed to go off to college and escape a difficult family situation at the same time.

JoeAnn left her department-store job in 1977 and began working seven hours a day for a Catholic social-service agency. CoDe North was operated by the Covenant of the Holy Names in North Memphis, and its focus was on refurbishing houses in the area to provide alternative low-income housing. For two years she was a CoDe North community organizer ("really a go-fer person," JoeAnn says), helping secure donations, finding students and other volunteers to work in the summer refurbishing program, and running around town doing whatever the CoDe North staff needed.

Working seven hours a day made for a tight schedule, but it allowed her to drop her children off at school, and she could go home at lunch hour and cook dinner so it would be ready for the kids; her mom would finish watching the meal.

That same year Monroe graduated from the University of Memphis with a master's in education. He proudly reported his degree to the local board of education and soon saw a salary increase of $142 a month—a small fortune at the time. He journaled that "I felt like my hard work paid off not just in my salary but because my degree helped me to improve my daily classroom teaching."

Over the next thirty years, he taught sixth grade, with a particular focus on science. He was the kind of teacher that children truly loved, and they showed it. Before Christmas vacation, Monroe's students always brought him presents. Monroe made it clear to the kids that no presents were needed, but they always wanted to honor him, to give back to the man who gave them so much.

One Christmas when he was teaching at a white school, Monroe noticed a little girl looking distressed as she watched the other kids bring him gifts. He knew she came from an extremely poor family and barely had enough food to eat, much less money for a present for him. Monroe's truck, loaded with produce, was a common sight in North Memphis as he drove through neighborhoods giving away food to people who couldn't get to the store or whose cabinets were bare at the end of the month. The thought had occurred to him to bring food to this girl's family, but as a southern black man, he knew better than to show up at a white house with food . . . which would never be eaten.

As other children handed him their presents wrapped in bright Christmas paper, he saw the girl pull a calendar from her desk and get busy, erasing and erasing until it was almost like new. Then she rolled it up, tied a string around it, and walked up to hand it to him, so proud that she had a gift.

Monroe knelt down and opened his giant hand so the little girl could place her humble gift in it.

"Thank you very much!" he told her as tears rolled down his cheeks. He knew what it was like to have nothing, and he never forgot where he came from.

Towards the end of the 1970s, the limelight shone brightly on the Ballards. They were showered with recognition, including the Memphis Newspaper Guild Citizens of the Year Award. At the ceremony acknowledging the couple as the Optimist Citizens of the Year, Mayor Wyeth Chandler presented them with the keys to the city.

One of JoeAnn's accomplishments was finding grants for a young man who wanted to go to college. JoeAnn had seen a woman weeping in the grocery store and asked what was wrong. "My son is so smart, and he wants to go to college, but we can't afford it," the woman sobbed. JoeAnn found the money.

When the news reporter asked JoeAnn how long she and her husband planned to mentor and parent the children of perfect strangers, she replied, "It's not like a job you get tired of and quit. We'll do it until we're not needed, so it probably will be for the rest of our lives."

The following year, they received the Congressional Community Service Award and a two-month-long "Salute to Mr. and

Mrs. Ballard" from the Memphis chapter of Operation PUSH.

The photo in a 1978 news clip shows ten-year-old Ephie and little Linda in white short-sleeved shirts and crisp, solid-color A-line skirts that look to be cut from the same cloth and made from the same pattern. Linda's skirt is fitted with crisscrossed suspenders to hold up the skirt that once may have been her big sister's. The girls are busy at the sink, their hair neatly pulled back. Ora Mae, in a solid-color dress, is poised with a serving dish in her hands, about to take it from the kitchen to the dining room. Her eyes are on toddler Monroe Jr., who stands behind his mother. JoeAnn commands the kitchen from the stove. The photographer has succeeded in catching the feel of the Ballard home: efficient, inclusive, nourishing.

As the article points out, the Ballards were still in the process of remodeling their home to accommodate more children. Monroe and whatever friends would help him were slowly turning the attic into four more bedrooms with a double bath. The Memphis Area Planning and Design Center contributed architectural ideas, but the Ballards had run out of money. Because of the article, a little more help trickled in. Bit by bit, they completed the upstairs renovations and soon filled the space with four girls.

Their home was bursting at the seams, averaging eleven children on any given day. Some were with them full-time, others lived with them on weekends or spent Sundays with them. Since their work often required travel, the Ballards bought first a large trailer and then a motor home that would allow the whole family and a few extra kids to travel together. This allowed Monroe and JoeAnn to be hands-on parents at all times and also gave their children a chance to experience ministry on a daily basis.

When a white boy was sent over, they sprang to action to make room for him. Tom's two sisters had already gotten pregnant and dropped out of school. He had been shipped off to his stepfather while his mother tried to rebuild her life, but he was getting into trouble and challenging his stepfather's ability to manage the seventeen year-old. Although JoeAnn did not have the means to take a teenaged boy into their girls-only house, they let him stay in the motor home for a couple of months until he turned eighteen, found a job, and secured his own place to live.

JoeAnn made it her business to know not only the children's parents but also who was in the community and who had resources and talents to give. She got to know the doctors, lawyers, politicians, and the common people in Memphis. She spent many hours walking to offices, explaining her mission, building relationships. She found free food, she asked for paper for her newsletter, she found summer jobs for any child who was old enough to work. Her own work was nonstop; for every need she filled, another one rose.

"We were rotating kids right and left. Two hundred and fifty kids were coming to the Christmas party. We were offering outreach to parents and families, giving away food to people who showed up at the door, and running all of this out of our pockets. When we had eleven girls staying with us, we saw that we had reached our maximum. Financially we couldn't handle any more. The accountant who was helping us said, 'If you do one more thing, you're going to go bankrupt.' He didn't know we were picking up cans to get the money from recycling, doing everything we could. I asked people, 'If you are throwing anything away, tell me first. I don't care what you're giving away. Let me have it.'"

The city-county public information system catalogued the Ballards in a category of their own: not a nonprofit institution or an agency or a for-profit company, just a nice married couple who could be counted on to provide food, clothing, household articles, "and assistance, whatever type of personal help is needed."

That Memphis public listing kick-started their widespread availability as public speakers. From that point on, Monroe and JoeAnn rose to the call and traveled across the city to inspire others to help, regardless of how small the household income was, regardless of the size of the home. The Ballards were only available to speak after six o'clock during the week because they both worked and hosted a family dinner each night for a dozen or so children.

Although Monroe and JoeAnn were busier than ever, they still remained attentive parents to their three children—and years later to their four children, after Justin Blake Ballard was added to their family. Justin was born in 1986.

With so many demands on their time, they knew that if they weren't careful, their own children could fall through the cracks.

"I knew the common scenario of the 'preacher's kid,' or any child of parents in ministry, who rebelled against his or her up-bringing," JoeAnn said. "We did not want our kids to feel that ministry was more important to us than they were. And we didn't try to shield them from the unpleasant parts of ministry, because we wanted them to see a real ministry with a real God at the helm. They witnessed the frustrations of not having enough money and of cooking meals to feed so many mouths, but, more importantly, they saw that God always provides. Living in such close quarters on the road, our children were being discipled."

It was only natural that, at times, the Ballard's biological chil-dren would struggle to share their parents and their home with others. On one of Ephie's birthdays, all she wanted was to for her parents to take her out—without any other kids. Her wish was granted: Monroe and JoeAnn spent the day taking Ephie where she wanted to go . . . but at the end of the day, their elder daughter was ready to go home. She didn't feel right not sharing the day with others.

One family trip became a defining moment for every member.

After noticing a dramatic increase in the number of home-less people in Memphis, the Ballards visited a Washington, D.C., church with an effective homeless program. After showing the Ballards their facility and operations, a group of people from the church held a prayerful meeting with Monroe, JoeAnn, and their children. The Washington church members described what they felt God had shown them about the direction of the Ballards' ministry in Memphis.

Looking back, JoeAnn believes that trip marked Ephie's initial understanding and inspiration that she would one day lead the organization her parents had unintentionally started.

Back in their motor home that night, Ephie said to the other children, "Don't say a word about what happened today. This was very important, and it's a secret. God is doing something big, and y'all had better keep your mouths shut."

SEVEN
A Light in the Dark

BY THE LATE '70S, MONROE AND JOEANN HAD maxed out the services they could offer in their own home. They had their biological children, full-time foster children, weekend foster children, and a house full of donated items that were constantly streaming in. While the Ballards began to wonder how they would continue to meet such vast needs with limited space, they were attracting the attention of a small cadre of prominent Christian Memphians: Larry Lloyd, Rev. Billy Joe Jackson, Charlotte Worley, and Jon Abercrombie.

Lloyd worked closely with the poor through the Young Life Urban organization and had rocked a few boats with his hands-on, up-close approach to creating change. Worley and Abercrombie worked for Youth Guidance, an urban division of Youth for Christ, and Jackson was regional coordinator for Prison Fellowship Ministries, also an evangelical nonprofit. These individuals and the groups they represented were doing what they could, but they all had a vision for what they believed was really needed: a neighborhood-based ministry run by someone who was trusted and respected in the community. They knew just the person for the job.

Abercrombie and Lloyd took JoeAnn to lunch one day in June 1978 and shared their vision with her. They had secured a grant for $15,000 from the Second Presbyterian Church and wanted her to water and tend the seed they hoped would grow.

"JoeAnn was the perfect fit," Lloyd says. "She had a background of social service and Christian ministry, she had raised a bunch of kids, we knew about her work with CoDe North. We hired her on the spot. She jumped in not knowing if we were ever going to be able to fund the organization past the first year." But JoeAnn was, as Abercrombie says, "one of those forces of nature who will not give up."

Her grass-roots work for the previous twelve years, ministering to the community to meet urgent needs, had shown JoeAnn the necessity of foresight, planning, and fundraising, but she says, "I didn't know anything about ministry or about funding or having a staff. So I began to study everything Larry, Jon, Charlotte, and Billy Joe did . . . and I prayed."

Lloyd took JoeAnn with him to training conferences and to visit similar agencies. He coached her in leadership and networking. For the next nine months as the newly named Northside Christian Center was coming into being, JoeAnn saw for the first time the inner workings of a Christian human-services organization.

Lloyd also tutored JoeAnn in raising money, but JoeAnn recognized she would have to hand-fashion her own fundraising tools.

"It wasn't going to work for a black woman to go around Memphis asking rich white people for money," she says. "These were powerful white men who were major donors. They were calling their friends and saying, 'John, we need $15,000. Can you make a donation?' I knew I couldn't do that. Fred Davis, a black insurance man, was the only man in Memphis I personally knew that had any money, and he was already giving. I wasn't born with a silver spoon. I didn't know anyone who had any windfalls. I didn't know anyone with money. I had to figure out how an African American woman would lead an organization in Memphis, Tennessee."

The Northside Christian Center was given office space in the basement of the Old Decatur Christian Church at Decatur and Breedlove, and the pastor of the church was appointed to the board. North Memphis was known for having a high crime rate, but the gang violence that went *unreported* was tragic. It is no coincidence that, since those days, North Memphis has produced

hundreds of hip-hop rappers whose lyrics revolve around gun violence, prostitution, drugs, and murder.

To prepare JoeAnn for the work, the board of directors sent
her straight into one of the poorest, most violent, most crime-
ridden public housing projects in the country: Cabrini-Green in
Chicago.

JoeAnn rode a Trailways bus for more than ten hours, 500 miles
north, to Cabrini-Green. The people who would train her were af-
filiated with Young Life and other Christian groups working to
make a difference in a project that most leaders had completely
given up on. A few brave ones had gone so far as to move into
the neighborhood and spent time with residents to try to build
relationships.

JoeAnn and the other young people in training lived in a college dorm in another neighborhood and were closely protected
from the worst of Cabrini-Green, but every day for two weeks she
rode the train into Chicago's gangland. Five thousand poor people
were living—if you could call it that—in a tight cluster of high-
rise and midrise towers.

Some of the neighborhood corners tolled as many as fifty murders a year.

As gang violence escalated, more police offers died in gun-
fire exchanges with gangsters, who often wielded more powerful
weapons.

Policemen became targets.

When two policemen were assassinated walking across a
Cabrini-Green baseball field, law enforcement took a defensive
stance and simply began scaling back patrols.

City leaders, frustrated at their impotency in the face of drug
violence, made life even less human for Cabrini-Green residents
by simply paving over many of the unkempt lawns, leaving a concrete wasteland. Apartments that had caught fire from drug manufacturing or been burned during gang violence were boarded up
and left unrepaired. Streetlights went out, or were shot out, and

neighborhoods left in the dark. Garbage pick-up was scaled back, leaving residents with the constant presence of trash, the smell of filth and decay, and a rising infestation of rats and roaches.

Returning to Memphis, JoeAnn had seen the worst—but she had also seen the best in the people who dedicated their lives to bring light to a darkened time and place. Since she was a little girl she had prayed for God's guidance, but returning from Cabrini-Green she prayed specifically: *You got to help me now, Lord. Show me how I can help the people of North Memphis.*

Within days, a local businessman called and offered her a surplus from his store.

"I've got five thousand gold shoestrings. Come 'n' get 'em."

Young JoeAnn wondered what in the world she would do with such a donation but soon realized it might be part of the answer to her prayer.

Looking over all those packs of shoestrings, an idea burst into her head. She had already planned to survey neighborhood folks to figure out what kind of services the new center would need to offer. Now she had a reward for them!

She typed out an easy questionnaire, made five hundred copies, bought a set of wooden pencils, sharpened them, and set out on foot early the next morning.

Walking up and down the streets, JoeAnn approached people with a smile and asked them gently if they would please give their opinion on what people needed most from the NCC. Sometimes she filled out the survey for a mother holding her babies or a man who had dropped out of school.

Any adult completing a survey was given a set of gold shoelaces for each child in their home. In an area with few resources and no money for fancy extras, JoeAnn quickly became the most sought-after newcomer in the neighborhood. Folks looked for her, hoping for a chance to get shoelaces. Gold shoestrings became the new status symbol, and with them JoeAnn had opened a door that others would walk through for decades to come.

The next week the Northside Christian Center officially opened its doors with a clothes closet and food pantry, filled with all the items people had specified on surveys.

It was a good start: she had an office, critical supplies to offer, and folks were beginning to find her. But not all of them had the best intentions. The Old Decatur Christian Church was a rambling old building with a dwindling congregation in what was known as "a bad part of town."

At one point there had been hundreds of regular parishioners, but the general degradation of the neighborhood had caused many to flee to safer neighborhoods. Having a smaller number of its own congregants, the church now rented out space to other denominations for their programs and services. With so many people coming and going throughout the week, nobody took much notice of who came and went through the doors—or the windows.

JoeAnn worked alone in the basement, her office behind one of more than a dozen doors off a long hallway. Here, she made phone calls and organized resources. On her third day at work, she heard something bang against the door of her office and crash into the hallway. Heart racing, she rushed to lock the door and stood to the side.

No more sounds came for a while.

But just as she had settled down to work again, something else crashed against the door. Two male voices were cursing and laughing. They made frightening, ugly sounds before eventually leaving.

That night as she lay down in bed beside her husband, she wanted to tell him. They told each other everything.

This time, she didn't.

She didn't want him to worry. And although she went to work every day with a little pocket of fear in her heart, she never told anyone about her dread. She didn't want anyone to tell her that she shouldn't be the director of the Northside Christian Center. She had work to do there, and she planned to do it—come what may.

The disruptions continued nearly every day.

JoeAnn walked into the church looking over her shoulder, locked all the outside doors behind her, locked her office door, and tried to ignore the sounds she heard in the hallway. She soon began finding her office completely trashed in the mornings; her tormenters were crawling into the building through broken windows and doors that wouldn't properly shut and lock. Not only did they destroy her paperwork and throw office supplies on the floor, but they also urinated in her desk drawer.

Her problem was two high-school dropouts who lived in the neighborhood. Most people would have probably just continued to lock the doors and hide or possibly even given up and left, but JoeAnn's approach to the crisis was consistent with the way she lived her life. She faced the problem head-on by finding out where the boys lived and introducing herself to their parents, without ever saying a word about the problems their sons were causing her.

Every weekday after work, JoeAnn walked through the neighborhood to the boys' parents' houses and sat on the porch talking with them. She made a point of noticing and asking what the family needed, and she began bringing them donated items. If family members were out of work, she tried to find them jobs. When the two boys came around, she spoke uplifting words and encouraged them to get back in school. She offered to take them to church. Little by little, she became their trusted friend. The vandalism and the terrorism stopped.

Throughout the community JoeAnn's style was to work intimately.

She sat down with people, looked them in the eyes, showed up consistently, asked them what they needed, listened to them, and always returned with help of some kind—even if that help was just to sit a little longer.

"You can never underestimate the power of presence," she says, and her effectiveness with people is all the evidence one could want. She won the respect of the entire North Memphis community. She reached out to them, and they responded to her. She was changing lives, one by one.

Because of the focus on individual neighborhoods, the name of the agency was changed to the Neighborhood Christian Center (NCC).

From the time JoeAnn was hired to run the center's daily operations in 1979, she remained its sole employee for the next six years.

Two part-time employees were eventually hired, though Joe-Ann remained the only full-time employee for the following ten years. While she was the only full-time employee, Monroe was always around, volunteering his time and working as hard as any full-time staffer.

As the work grew and they were called to reach more lives, Joe-Ann continued to lean on her husband. They were always a team, picking up donations together many evenings of the week after eating dinner with their family.

The center's growth came quickly.

As Eddie Foster, a longtime board member, recalls, "All of a sudden we had vans and a payroll, and we were barely managing. I had sleepless nights wondering how we were going to make payroll. But JoeAnn had a conviction that God would provide. She'd say, 'I'm gonna pray about it.' Her first instinct in times of need is to pray. That has always inspired me."

Although JoeAnn knew how to pray, she didn't feel that she had the business background she needed to properly run an organization.

The first chairman of the board, Frank Fourmy, became her self-appointed mentor. Fourmy, a wealthy businessman, helped her fashion a model of effective ministry practices that were also good business practices.

At the time JoeAnn had already seen too many ministries that had lost respect and trust in the community because they didn't have a clear vision or didn't convey that vision to every staff member.

Searching for one word to describe her approach, she settles on *integrity*.

As the staff grew, JoeAnn preached the same message to her employees that she chanted to herself: everything that came into the NCC was to be used for the good of the community.

"I wanted us to be as intentional as a company like FedEx that lives up to what it guarantees. When they don't make the delivery overnight, they are the first ones to admit it and to give you your money back. They know that their success rests on their word."

She knew that the NCC needed to be consistent, available, and honor its commitments. She created a policy that the NCC would be open from 7:59 a.m. to 5:01 p.m. to give clients a little flexibility in receiving services. She also required that staff submit regular reports, accurate records, and stay in constant communication with clients. While incorporating good business practices, JoeAnn maintained a clear focus on the NCC as ministry.

Watching closely how the NCC conducted business and served its community, donors with longstanding concern about the problems in Memphis began to funnel resources into the community through the NCC.

Checks filtered in from individuals as well as foundations.

The First Evangelical Church matched the Presbyterian's starter gift of $15,000 and kept the NCC on its list of supported organizations.

The Clarence Day Foundation sent a $4,000 check to the local Sears department store for the Neighborhood Christian Center to buy Christmas presents for the children who came to the annual Christmas party.

"Many people say that the poor should not receive help from others because it might foster laziness and dependence," JoeAnn says. "I have heard that it's easier for an animal shelter to raise money than a homeless shelter. Animals are simple, their needs are clear, and no one blames them when there are difficulties in their lives. But with people in distress, our reactions are much more complicated. I don't know how many times I've heard some-one say, 'Why can't he just get a job?'"

But many Americans who *are* in the labor force are extremely poor. A 2011 study from the U.S. Bureau of Labor document-ed 46.2 million Americans living at or below the poverty line (a family of four people living on $22,350 annual income). Many of them are the working poor. These numbers reflect people— statistically, women, blacks, and Hispanics—who are stuck in low-paying part-time jobs. Many of America's poor actually are work-ing while the vast majority of the rest are caught in the vicious cycle of welfare.

In the land of opportunity, it's easy to assume that every Amer-ican has the same chance at "life, liberty, and the pursuit of hap-piness." For many, though, it's not as simple as pulling themselves up by their bootstraps. What if you don't have bootstraps to begin with? What if having no car means you can't get to work, a sick child means you lose your job—your part-time job that doesn't provide sick days? What if finally getting out of the welfare system means you no longer get any childcare assistance, and new child-care costs while you work put you right back where you started?

Most middle-class Americans are familiar with circumstantial poverty, a temporary period of financial hardship. But generation-al poverty, the no-bootstraps kind of poverty, is nearly impossible to fathom—unless it has happened to you or someone very close to you.

As Amanda Opelt wrote about her first encounter with urban poverty: "Like many Americans, I felt a certain sense of indiffer-ence towards poor in America, and there was maybe, buried deep in my subconscious, even a mild contempt."

Opelt concluded that one of our country's biggest crises is "the cycle of generational poverty . . . a bankruptcy of spirit, a deficit of hope. It is poverty of education, community, safety, health, and spiritual guidance."

The ill-informed attitude that the poor are lazy was and is one of the biggest obstacles JoeAnn faced as she tried to persuade others to work alongside her.

From her own experiences as an abandoned child who was taken in and cared for, she knew that effective help could change the course of a life. "I was determined to train my staff to give in a way that helped rather than hindered the disadvantaged."

One of the ways she did this was to draw from her own experiences of being pulled out of what would certainly have been a life of generational poverty and into a life of community and hope. The people the NCC was serving, with rare exception, came from generational poverty, with their only real safety nets being social aids like food stamps and Medicaid.

Looking back on her own life, JoeAnn recognizes that her safety nets were numerous and strong: her foster parents who took her in at their own financial sacrifice, students and teachers in West Virginia who showed her real lives of faith, the kind neighbor in Memphis who gave her a place to live, the Memphis leaders who believed in her and gave her a chance, her husband who was her constant partner in all things.

A black girl born without boots or bootstraps, JoeAnn's life had been lifted up by others.

She had learned that the only way to effect lasting change in the lives of those in need was to become a surrogate community for them.

To become:
the resource they never had,
the friend they never knew,
the positive voice they never heard,
the math tutor they never had,
the spiritual mentor they never knew.

It's complicated, and it can be messy, as Opelt observed, "but Jesus never seemed to mind a mess, and no one he ever healed or scolded or cried for or embraced had a simple story."

Creating change isn't a tidy business, and JoeAnn believes the only way to go about it is to blend church ministry with human services.

The NCC engaged people's hearts in order to change their lives. Sometimes the first step is to meet immediate needs . . . but only as a way to build a relationship.

JoeAnn trained her staff to use new eyes in seeing their clients. People, she told them, are much more than a set of behaviors.

The work is to first create stability in lives so that change and growth can occur. Only with a safety net in place can adversity and struggle be a platform to growth.

As JoeAnn's ministry philosophy became reality, central operations for the NCC—which consisted of JoeAnn and the two part-time employees, including a half-time assistant—moved into a house at 745 Looney Street.

Her assistant was a seventeen-year-old who had managed to graduate from high school despite the death of both parents. Like most people who would come to work for the NCC, she came with a need and became part of the organization's family.

They set up offices in two front rooms. The rest of the house was used for direct services.

On Tuesdays they offered a mother's day out for four hours.

They created an after-school club for neighborhood children.

They equipped the kitchen and made it available to anyone who needed to cook a meal for themselves. And they passed the word that any child who was hungry or who needed to get away from home for a while could come in, sit and talk, and eat.

The bedrooms were for people who needed a place to stay—some were homeless, some were in between homes as they transitioned from high school into the workforce, some simply needed a refuge from a difficult family situation for a few days. It was JoeAnn's first attempt at offering interim housing outside of her own home.

Setbacks were inevitable.

One woman who came to them for help was homeless, on welfare, and had a little girl. JoeAnn had furnished the entire NCC house with donated and solicited items, including a clothes washer and dryer. JoeAnn gave the woman an orientation, showing her the house and explaining that she could stay for as long as three months. She went so far as to tell the woman that she was free to take all the furniture with her, except for the washer and dryer, when she moved out.

The woman repaid the agency's kindness by loading all the furniture and appliances, including the washer and dryer, into a truck in the middle of the night, while no one else was in the house, and driving away without a word of thanks.

Wanting to believe the best but unwilling to foster a thief, Joe-Ann called one of the NCC board members, Jim Witherington, and explained that her guest must have misunderstood what she was allowed to take and not take.

She and Witherington made a plan to show up in person at the place JoeAnn figured the woman had gone. They would talk to her and try to retrieve the washer and dryer. After all, JoeAnn had helped her for the last three months; surely she would be amenable to returning the appliances for others to use.

Witherington and JoeAnn climbed into his new Dodge truck and parked at the house, which stood in a low-rent part of town. Walking toward the front door, they saw the woman appear in the doorway holding a .45 revolver and warning, "If you come any closer, I'll blow your heads off."

"Jim jumped completely over his truck, and we both started running up the street," JoeAnn laughs, remembering that day.

"We had to get the police to go back with us that afternoon to get Jim's truck. Needless to say, we left the washer and dryer and never went back to ask for it again!"

While the memory is now funny, there have been many times when the deceit, dishonesty, and ingratitude of the recipients of such love and care were very discouraging and even painful.

Personal tragedy also took its toll on the young woman who

devoted herself to helping others.

She had been pregnant—a joyous event for her and Monroe—but the baby had been born dead. It was an August day when she lay in a hospital room recovering from surgery and praying for the infant whose life was so short.

"I was in a great deal of pain," she recalls, "and I remember answering the phone with a weak voice. The voice on the other end said, 'Hello, Mrs. Ballard. I heard you were in the hospital and wanted to see how you're doing.'"

JoeAnn was moved to think that this person who had been a recipient of her help was now caring for her.

This sentiment soon changed, however, as the person offered her condolences and in the same breath asked if the NCC could pay her overdue utility bill.

"My heart sank," JoeAnn says. "I thought a client was responding to *my* needs when in reality, she was concerned about her own. As I made calls to ensure that this client would not have her electricity shut off, I realized that my life was indeed not my own. That I could never have a single thought for what I might receive in turn. I understood why clients behaved as they did at times. If I had been poor my whole life, I would probably behave in a similar fashion."

While she understood the sentiments behind dishonesty, she could also recognize a scam a mile away and wouldn't allow it to happen. JoeAnn and Monroe established checkpoints to verify the legitimacy of their clients' needs. If a person said he was from a certain place and ran out of gas, they checked the license plates on the car. If someone said she needed money for gas to get to a doctor's appointment, a call would be put in to the doctor's office to verify the story.

In the initial years, the NCC supported the needy from one crisis to the next. The needs were valid—and often completely overwhelming.

"We were not changing those situations," JoeAnn says. "The

food, clothes, and utility assistance were simply a bridge to hold people up and keep them from falling deeper into poverty and despair. Until time changed their circumstances."

She compares crisis ministry to an airplane biding its time in a holding pattern, waiting for weather to improve.

"The first time I was on an airplane," she recalls, "I woke up and I thought the plane was standing still. It was circling in the sky for over an hour while a storm passed below. I sat on that plane thinking of the NCC. In ministering to the poor, we are moving all the time but not always reaching a destination. Yet we are called to be caregivers in the waiting, much like the flight attendant who continued to bring peanuts, coffee, and kind words until the plane could land." JoeAnn and Monroe learned over the years that meeting the practical needs of the poor was often like that: bumpy and often seemingly hopeless but with brief periods when clients could be guided into better conditions."

When the needs were real, the NCC staff moved quickly and with what can only be called grace. Kedra Jones, NCC's longtime compassionate-ministries director, has worked face to face with the nitty-gritty of human suffering.

"When people come to us, they have already called their family members and been through their churches. They are destitute," she says. "One lady came to us after calling all over Memphis for help," she recalls. "Her son had been shot, and she had all but $150 of the hospital bill. We were able to give that to her."

Handwritten thank-you notes from clients have always been plentiful on Kedra's desk. Some needs have been a matter of survival; others are a matter of human dignity.

I thank God every time I remember you, one woman wrote. "We were able to help her bury her sister," Kedra explains. "If there's going to be a funeral, you're also going to need clothes, so we made sure she knew about the clothes closet."

While some people came looking for a handout, others haven't known how to ask for what they need. One young woman came on a cold December day, saying she needed some warm clothes. It turned out that sixteen people lived in her one-bedroom apartment; she needed much more than warm clothes!

JoeAnn taught her growing staff that it was up to them to look into the souls of the forgotten and provide the right kind of food.

"A lot of the time when they come for clothing, it's not for clothes; they really need the lady in the clothes room to pray with them. When people say, 'I have a need,' that is their point of entry," she reflects. "That's our cue to look deeper to see what's going on. It's like a person who is thirty-five-years-old and says, 'I'm always tired.' The doctor is going to start checking for disease. If a person is coming into our ministry looking for clothing, I'm looking at you, and I see that you don't have a job, you're disabled, maybe you're discouraged, and that has created a spirit of laziness in you; but the real need has to be discovered in order to properly serve the person."

In 1981 the NCC moved to 735 North Parkway, just one street over from Looney. Even in this short of a distance, the area was darker—overrun with liquor stores, pawnshops, and buildings with signs advertising "private parties." It was just the kind of place that needed an organization like the Neighborhood Christian Center.

JoeAnn was still the only full-time employee at this point, but slowly, as some of her tasks were being passed onto others, she was able to expand her focus. The organizational vision grew and solidified, especially after Monroe's retirement from teaching when he joined JoeAnn at the NCC full-time.

Until that point, everything they had done for the "kids" had come out of their own personal money. By 1978, with the center raising its own money, the Ballards no longer had to use their own small incomes to help. Monroe collected a retirement check, Social Security, and the center paid him a small stipend.

Together, they were an unstoppable force of compassion in the city. With more money coming in, JoeAnn was able to hire a tutoring coordinator to run the after-school programs and a driver to round up donated items, relieving JoeAnn and Monroe of the demanding pick-up schedule they had kept for years.

Even with a small staff supporting them now, JoeAnn and Monroe still needed more help to meet all the demands—a lot more help. They needed volunteers, and, thankfully, just as funding increased, so did the number of people who respected the NCC and wanted to give of their time through such an organization.

The idea of volunteering was a foreign one to JoeAnn because, as she says, "many black people worked two or three jobs and didn't have time to volunteer. Volunteering was something I thought only white women did in hospitals. My conception of volunteers was that they were privileged people who did something for others only to feel good about themselves."

Fortunately she soon learned that she was wrong. One of the first activities started by the NCC was a tutoring program, and when volunteers began to come after work and on Saturday mornings, week after week, she had to rethink her stereotypes. She reflects, "They were showing up every week and struggling with these kids and loving these kids in very tangible ways. I began to see that we weren't doing this alone."

Many people over the years have been so committed to the NCC that they are more like staff than volunteers. Debbie, a young lady who began helping at Christmas when thousands of boxes of food are packed and delivered to needy families, became very close with a family the NCC was serving. She began tutoring one of the children and has followed that family closely for years. Every Sunday she would take the kids out to eat, and on Thursday nights she had a Bible study with them. One of the young men from that family is now driving for the transit authority and is a devout Christian. One of the girls saved money to buy a house. The family is still poor, but they have hope. They have had Debbie to model true faith and wise decisions for them. This type of scenario has played out numerous times over the years.

As many lives that have been changed through the help of volunteers, just as many volunteers have had their lives changed through their relationships with the socio-economically poor. Joe-Ann recalls what Memphis was like during the recession in the early 1980s when day after day more clients were walking through the doors with heavy problems.

"One volunteer in particular assisted me in interviewing these clients to see what type of help they needed," she says. "During an interview with a client, she got out of her chair, walked out the door, and didn't come back. For days, I called her but couldn't get her to talk about what was bothering her. After about three weeks, she told me it was more than she could handle to see one person after another with serious obstacles." JoeAnn knew how she felt, but she also knew from her own background that no life, no situation, is hopeless.

Growing up in Lucedale, having been raised by people who never questioned taking her in and bringing her into their community, it was more natural for JoeAnn to do what she could about a situation rather than just feel terrible about it. Just as she needed to train her staff, she recognized that she must teach volunteers and donors how to move past guilt-driven service and giving and into gratitude-driven service and giving. The first step was for Joe-Ann to deal with her own pride, which made it difficult for her to receive help from supporters. "I was afraid people would think I was begging, always holding out my hand for more help," she says, "but eventually I saw that these were people who really wanted to give, whether I had my hand out or not."

She also began to realize that for the NCC to become a true community of giving and receiving, supporters needed to be ministered to as well. JoeAnn began calling them, writing letters, making visits, and praying for them. When a youth group came to volunteer, she would observe to see if any teen was isolated and build into that one. When in-kind gifts were given, she made it a point to learn the circumstances behind the gift if possible.

A woman died who had been a faithful prayer supporter of the NCC, and her daughter gave some of her mother's recipes to JoeAnn. The recipes reflected the mother's lifestyle; they were economical, nutritious, and simple. JoeAnn understood the spirit in which they were given, and in honor of the deceased supporter shared her recipes with clients who were young mothers. Her daughter was so thankful that her mother's ministry was living on even after her death.

It was clear to JoeAnn and Monroe that God had not called them to operate a "charity." JoeAnn clarifies, "To give clothes to a charity meant that they would go to meet a need. To donate clothes to the NCC meant that both the giver and recipient would be blessed."

In *Good News to the Poor*, Theodore W. Jennings offers stalwart agreement with the Ballards. "Breaking down the barriers between the givers and the receivers of aid, between those who have and those who have not, is an essential expression of the solidarity that liberates the privileged from their blindness and the marginalized from their invisibility."

To deepen their own understanding of their mission, the Ballards studied the book of Acts, in which the early church shared all things in common. JoeAnn knew from firsthand experience the difference between charity and "sharing all things in common."

In this way the Basin community and the early church are similar. It was difficult to make class distinctions if you grew up in Basin. JoeAnn had a Lawrence cousin who was a very successful farmer and could easily have lived in a fancy house, but instead he chose to live in his modest childhood home. This is typical in that community.

"You would never know from one house to the next what people really have," says JoeAnn. "Ownership is important, but acquiring wealth isn't. It's about being a good steward in the community in order to guarantee the well-being of every person rather than the wealth of a few."

They prayed that this principle found in both Basin and the early church would become a reality at the NCC—and they began to see some beautiful answers to that prayer. "People gave of their best rather than pants from ten years ago with holes in them," says JoeAnn. "Most of our donors had more than they needed at the time, so they chose to share their investments with others. The recipients saw the quality of the donations and shared in the investments as they used the items with pride. The clothes they wore from the closets of others became a means to getting a job or attending church rather than just a handout."

The surrogate community JoeAnn had envisioned was coming to pass.

EIGHT
To Every Thing There is a Season

A T THE REQUEST OF NCC BOARD MEMBER
Frank Jemison, JoeAnn opened an office in a troubled
housing development in 1995. Jemison had bought the apartment
complex, whose residents were mostly single mothers, and he knew
JoeAnn could bring a sense of unity to a splintered community. It
became the first satellite branch of the NCC.

People had lived quietly in Binghampton until the city of
Memphis incorporated it and drove a highway through the heart
of the town. What had once been a thriving community became a
ghost town. Vacated buildings stood alone and unnoticed by cars
speeding past on the interstate. Crime and drug use soared as did
the murder rate, with an especially disturbing trend of drive-by
shootings from cars on the highway.

The first day as JoeAnn moved in a few pieces of office furniture and supplies, no one bothered her, and she worked alone all
day. She would have been glad to speak to the neighbors, but no
one was around. Every apartment and home seemed locked up
tight, with the windows closed and the shades drawn. On Joe-
Ann's second day, she heard an awful noise and walked outside to
find a man lying on the concrete alongside the building, bleeding
to death. The victim, who had multiple stab wounds, died before
an ambulance arrived. Murders had become a weekly occurrence
in the area.

In an effort to combat the escalating violence and the resulting
fear of the residents, JoeAnn organized weekday services for chil-

dren in the new NCC space, then spread the word in the neighborhood. She offered tutoring and snacks after school and in the summertime and lunch every day for any child who was home. The environment she created became a safe haven for people in the area, and they once again began to unlock their doors and lift their shades.

"Within one year, the killings had all but stopped," she says. "My husband would get a call at two in the morning and drive out there. We made it hard for those who were doing wrong by not turning our backs on their wrongdoing. We didn't run away in fear. Pretty soon they would leave." The program in Binghampton is still going strong and now feeds, tutors, and offers the love of Christ to forty to fifty kids a day.

The successes of the NCC opened the door for expansion into other neighborhoods, other cities, and even other states. "We didn't pick a city; the city picked us," JoeAnn says. "Somebody who worked with us would move to another area and say, 'Why don't we start one here?' I would go into the city once a week for ten months until I became familiar with what resources were there, get inroads for funding, raise the funds, and keep my ears to the ground for someone who could run it. We opened the NCC in Jackson, Mississippi, in 1989." Over the years, NCC sites have also opened in Decatur, Alabama, and Atlanta, Georgia.

By 1991 there were eleven NCC locations in various high-need Memphis neighborhoods—most in low-income housing complexes like the one in Binghampton, with eleven full-time and eight part-time employees and an estimated five hundred volunteers. At that time the Memphis locations served an estimated nine thousand families on an annual budget of $400,000.

As more sites were added, JoeAnn realized that she and Monroe couldn't be in all of those places at once, and their small staff and unpaid volunteers couldn't handle all the needs, either. Once again she turned to the book of Acts. She read that when Paul went out as a missionary, he always took others with him, and he always left people behind to carry on the work when he had to move on.

"He didn't try to do ministry alone," she says, "and he always filled in the spaces that he could not personally fill with those who were likeminded." She realized that the NCC needed other "missionaries" as well. God began to raise up people who lived in needy neighborhoods and wanted to serve but didn't have the resources to do so. JoeAnn asked these likeminded individuals to be "independent missionaries."

"Over the years," recalls JoeAnn, "we had distributed all the food, clothing, and other goods from one location, making it difficult to reach as many of the poor as we would like. The missionaries began to pick up and distribute goods out of their homes or churches, greatly increasing the number who received what they needed."

These people also knew their neighbors, so they knew the needs. Using this new method, within a few hours a whole truckload of donated food could be distributed in neighborhoods throughout the city. Because of the missionaries, hungry families who woke up with nothing to eat could go to bed full from a healthy supper of vegetables delivered by their own neighbors. This was another very powerful way to create community where before there had been none.

JoeAnn remembers an elderly man who has been an NCC missionary in his neighborhood for many years. He is uneducated and poor, but he loves his neighbors and wants to serve them. He has built relationships with a number of youths in his neighborhood. He picks up donations from the NCC and gives them to the families of those kids.

"We love it when older people become missionaries for the NCC because neighborhoods are desperate for wisdom and values that can only come from the elderly," says JoeAnn. "It was not enough for us to give food and clothes—we also needed values to be imparted, and older missionaries can do just that."

Just as older missionaries can fill an important role, the Ballards recognized that young people can serve their neighbors. Youth programs expanded into satellite sites, and out of those activities came kids with an interest in becoming teen missionaries. In response, the Ballards began to mentor compassionate teenagers to care for the practical and spiritual needs of their neighbors.

Mentoring this population wasn't an easy task.

Over the years JoeAnn explored the reasons why black youths growing up in the inner city can seem so callous toward others in their communities.

"Several decades after the end of slavery," she says, "African Americans began to push for education. We educated individuals at the cost of community. As a result, those individuals who received an education moved away from their communities. Inner-city youth moved to other cities and left their own behind. We had so trained them to achieve the 'American Dream' that the purpose of receiving an education was to acquire for themselves."

Understanding the history of inner-city problems was key in helping the Ballards dig deeply into the lives of teens as they trained them to restore not only their own lives but also their communities.

With more hands and feet carrying out the mission of the NCC throughout the city, more services were possible.

Summer programs for youths were started in various sites, giving children a safe place to go when they weren't in school.

A program Monroe had dreamed of for years began to take shape, providing students the opportunity to attend college. Kids who faithfully attended NCC after-school and summer programs could earn points that translated into dollars for scholarships, often allowing them to become the first ones in their families to go to college.

With the recession still taking a toll on the country in the early '90s, the Christmas Basket program was also started, which each year provided baskets of food to needy families the week before Christmas.

Eugene Cashman, who would eventually play a prominent role in the future of the NCC, recalls his first exposure to the Christmas Basket program—and to JoeAnn Ballard. Cashman and his wife, Kathy, were in Sunday school at the Second Presbyterian Church with Larry Jensen, who knew of the Ballards. Their Sunday-school class committed to raising money and goods for the Christmas Basket program.

In the spirit of the season, Cashman got his whole family involved in the project. On the day the baskets were to be handed out, Cashman, his wife, and their children went down to the distribution site. About three hundred baskets overflowing with food and gifts had been prepared.

"It was a humbling experience to see so many people who were so downtrodden waiting in line for baskets," Cashman says. "Most striking of all was that in order to receive a basket, there was a preliminary step people went through. A few NCC staff would gather around them and pray for them. Monroe, who was a bigger-than-life figure, was leading many of the volunteers. When I first saw JoeAnn, she was walking up and down the line of people with a yellow legal pad. I knew what she was doing: she was purging people from that line. She was looking for people who were just there to take but didn't have a need. She knew who they were. She was always gracious but firm. It was evident that she was the very embodiment of everything that I hold dear. A true pillar. And I could see that they wanted to empower people, not entitle them."

Today, through the hands of approximately 600 volunteers, the program serves ten thousand families with enough food in each basket to feed four meals to a family of four.

A new decade continued to bring tremendous growth and recognition of the work being done, often in unexpected ways. Trevecca Nazarene University awarded JoeAnn an honorary doctorate degree in 1991 in recognition of her service in Memphis. She was humbled by the recognition from a conservative, mostly white school in Nashville, but it merely heightened the overriding sense that God had a much larger plan at work through her life. She understood that any recognition that came her way was to be given back to God and that she must continue looking to Him to guide things.

More divine guidance came one Saturday in 1993 when Joe-Ann got a phone call from an unfamiliar male voice.

"Meet me at 223 Scott Street in an hour," the man said.

Fearless as always, she drove to the address and parked in front of a brick building that was obviously vacant. The stranger then gave JoeAnn a tour through the ground floor, which had been renovated for office space, and then downstairs to the full basement, which opened up to the driveway and was perfect for loading, unloading, and storage.

Once back outside, the man turned to JoeAnn and held out a set of keys.

"It's yours."

When the deed was signed over, JoeAnn learned that the former owner's name was Margaret Walker. Thus, the Walkers entered the cadre of those who did not seek recognition but merely sought to serve.

The Scott Street building was perfect for the growing organization. There was room enough for offices and plenty of warehouse space in the basement. JoeAnn, the administrative staff, and the warehouse staff moved into the Scott Street building while program operations remained at North Parkway. Appropriately, JoeAnn named the building that became the hub for the business side of things the C. Frank Fourmy Jr. Center.

The need for safe, low-income housing in Memphis was so persistent that both the Ballards and the NCC ventured into the affordable-housing business. The NCC launched its own housing program, the Neighborhood Housing Center, and bought the house next door to Monroe and JoeAnn's. This enabled them to place young men in the Ballard's care full-time.

Even though the young men lived in their own house, they strolled over to JoeAnn and Monroe's house for meals and nightly devotions. A joint effort between the Neighborhood Housing Center and Memphis Leadership Foundation established a new entity, the Neighborhood Housing Corporation, which built more than one hundred affordable homes over the next fifteen years.

One day in 1995 JoeAnn got a call from a neighbor saying, "If you've got $19,000, you can buy my grandparents' house."

The old couple who had lived in the home had passed away and bequeathed it to one of their grandchildren, who had let it fall into disrepair. JoeAnn and Monroe did not have that kind of money, but they had always operated on faith and weren't about to stop now. The bank loaned them the money, and they bought the house.

Studying on the greatest needs they saw, the Ballards knew exactly what to do next: create a home for single mothers.

"About twenty girls lived in that house over a five- to seven-year period," JoeAnn recalls, "and all of them got back on their feet, found community with each other and with us, either found jobs or got job training for the first time, and became better mothers."

After thirty years of serving as surrogate parents, Monroe and JoeAnn reached a prayerful conclusion that they would take no more foster children. The last three, Nicola, Janice and Susanne—students from Guyana—were in college and living with them on weekends, holidays, and summers.

As the Ballards moved away from foster parenting and the NCC continued to reach more and more neighborhoods, JoeAnn had a vision for a new building. The Frank Fourmy Center was perfect for distributing donations and for housing the staff members who worked closely with distribution, and the programs were doing well throughout the city, reaching the residents of low-income apartments. But there was no central location to offer programs to a large number of people from all over Memphis.

Up until this point the NCC had operated out of homes and small office spaces, which always limited the number of people who could be reached.

"When the Lord gave me the vision of the new building, it was just a piece of land in the middle of North Memphis. Every Saturday for a year, I would come over here and sit, rain or shine, and talk to God about how He might want us to use it. I never told anyone, not even my husband. After a year of that, I went to the board, and some of us came back to the site and prayed. The next week, a man came in and gave us a check for $1 million."

The name on the check was familiar: Ernest Bland Williams III—the man with the fancy handwriting, the closing attorney on the home she and Monroe had cared for so many children in, the man who had written a check for one hundred dollars for their Christmas party years earlier.

Williams led a life of privilege by anyone's standards: a graduate of Vanderbilt Law School who began his law practice at his father's well-established firm in Memphis. He was one of the original instructors at the University of Memphis School of Law and a faithful donor to various organizations that served Memphis's needy. He had followed JoeAnn's work from afar.

Just before his death in 2008, the Golightly Foundation founded by Williams gave the NCC the $1 million that kicked off a meticulously planned $4 million capital campaign amidst a long-lasting economic downturn. The rest of the money couldn't be raised without the campaign, but some would argue that neither could it be raised unless JoeAnn prayed on it.

A true pragmatist, Eddie Foster wasn't so sure the money would all come in for the ambitious campaign. "Building the new center seemed impossible to me," he says. "I remember walking around that lot and praying about it and hoping that would be something that God would provide in the way JoeAnn believed He would."

But few people knew exactly how much, or how fervently, JoeAnn prayed: throughout the day and into the night, through the sleepless hours and into the dawn.

Pray, pray, pray.

Pray unceasingly.

It took about a year to raise the remainder of the funds.

The capital campaign, their first, also marked the first time that JoeAnn said "yes" to government funds; the city of Memphis provided $250,000 in federal funding and an additional $50,000 for related expenses.

In 2004 the first shovel went in the ground at 785 Jackson Avenue in North Memphis. The central facility now stands as a true gem for both the impoverished neighborhood and the city. A massive building, covering 24,000 square feet, it is named the Golightly Building after its faithful and largest donor.

Life was good.

The beautiful building was built and paid for, children and families were streaming through the doors each day, donors and volunteers were investing in the ministry . . . and then, the unthinkable happened.

A decline in Monroe's health.

Monroe had been dealing with prostate cancer since an initial diagnosis in 2001. As the new millennium unfolded, he began to slow down for the first time. The change was gradual. Almost methodical . . . like the man himself.

His family and community helped him through the next seven years, to the extent that he would allow them.

During the last eighteen months of Monroe's life, he needed to be in bed. But he could not let go of the need to help with the center, so the family set up a bed for him right behind JoeAnn's office.

As Monroe Jr. notes with pride, "He would run his department from the bedside. Even when he went into the hospital, he still had something to say about operations. He never stopped going to work."

Monroe was still serving as the organization's director of operations until his admission to Baptist Memorial Hospital in Memphis, where he died two weeks later, on April 25, 2008.

More than eight hundred people streamed into the NCC chapel for his wake.

One by one, for hours, people stood and told the stories of how this man had affected their lives. How he had toiled with love in his heart, faced each day with faith and courage, never thinking of what was in it for himself.

In thirty years of teaching school at Douglass Elementary, Monroe never took a sick day. Under his tutelage, sixth-grade students at Douglass were assured of winning the citywide science fair. Before most people knew what ethanol was, Monroe's science students had made some in his class. If he gave a student a bad grade, he simultaneously requested a parent-teacher conference.

When not working with children at Douglass Elementary, Monroe had continued to mentor large numbers of children with JoeAnn, both in their own home and at the Neighborhood Christian Center. He taught them how to weld, paint, cut grass, engineer, rake leaves, organize and label *everything*, go to church, follow, lead, coach, train, wait, and love at all costs.

At Monroe's funeral service, his four children stood at the podium and named their favorite memories about their father: leading family devotions every night, teaching them how to ride a bike, how to drive a car.

Delivering one of many eulogies that day, Ephie's powerful voice cracked as she read aloud a letter of thanks from the four children to their father:

"Thank you, Daddy, for standing up through many of our meals. Our meals could include fifteen or twenty people at one time. We didn't realize that you were waiting to eat last to be sure there was enough food for everybody. Thank you for taking us on family vacations, year after year, and thank you for our special annual trip with Daddy, where you thought enough of each one of us to take us on a special one-on-one trip with you. Thank you for helping

128

us with our homework and for reminding us that it was our duty
to empower others so they could have a better quality of life."

Sitting behind the four Ballard children were rows of foster
children, some who had lived with the Ballards for years, some on
the weekends, and some for just a few days during a crisis.

Lee Stewart, who had been one of the white boys the Ballards
took into their home so many years earlier, stood before the crowd
and described his home life before moving in with JoeAnn and
Monroe.

"My father would get drunk and beat my mom. Sometimes I
would have to fight him off of her. I was so scared he was going to
hurt me when I went to sleep. I told Brother Monroe about it, and
he said, 'Come stay with my family at my house.' Even though
he didn't have enough room, he pulled a mobile home up to the
house, and I slept there. I never saw him upset. Once he hired me
to help paint a house. He left me alone, and when he came back,
I had made the biggest mess. Paint was everywhere. He just said,
'Lee, take a break.' When I came back from my break, he was
standing there with a paintbrush and a bucket and he said, 'We're
going to do this together.'"

Overwhelmed with emotion, Lee paused briefly before continuing.

"That was the moment that Monroe became my father. He had
the compassion in his heart to help everyone. I often wonder what
would have happened to me if the Ballards had never crossed the
racial lines and taken me in. After I married, every time Monroe
saw me he would ask me, 'How's your wife? How are your kids?'
And he would always end our talks with, 'I'm very proud of you.'"

Ester Britton and Ruby Bonds, two of JoeAnn and Monroe's
first foster children, also sat with family at Monroe's wake.

"We've come a long ways," Ester said. "Mr. and Mrs. Ballard
stood with me when nobody else would. They fed me, took me to
church, and I learned how to love God because of them. They put
me through school. They took out of their pockets to give to me

and my sister. Mr. Ballard wouldn't give up on me. He didn't care if you were a boy or girl, he'd say, 'Come on, we're gonna do an oil change,' or 'We're gonna change that flat tire.' He made sure I got my driver's license. He would tell you, 'Work hard for what you want in life.'" Before leaving the podium, Ester turned to Ephie, Linda, Monroe Jr., and Justin, and said, "I thank you for letting me share your father . . . I love him."

Among those in the room were the children of the foster kids, who themselves became the Ballards' surrogate grandchildren.

One of the last people to testify at his service was a graceful young woman who said, "I'm representing all the foster grandchildren. Will all the foster grandchildren please stand?"

At least two dozen people stood, some of them holding young children.

"Without Grandma and Grandpa Ballard and everyone else at the Neighborhood Christian Center, I wouldn't have been able to graduate from high school," the young woman said. "Grandpa Ballard was always there for me. Just last month, he was telling me I should go back and get my master's degree; I already have my bachelor's degree."

A giant of a man just like his father, Monroe Jr. grabbed the podium and recalled a few outstanding father-son memories, including learning to weld, constructing new walls, "raking the yard at two in the morning 'cause I forgot," he said with a smile.

Then with gravity, "If I can be half the man he is, I'll be all right. He had his own way of teaching. He had sayings, and sometimes I'd say, 'Where'd you get that from?' Those sayings of my father's are the stuff I'm drawing on now. He expected more from us. He told each one of us individually how proud he was of us. I don't know how he helped all those people because he was always there for us. He's left something for us to do: we have a mission."

NINE
Looking Back
to Move Forward

L OOKING BACK, IT SEEMS CLEAR THAT EPHIE'S life, beginning with her childhood, had been building up to this point. Her parents had talked with her about taking the reins at the NCC as they grew older. Now that the moment had come, it seemed like too much; but she remembered the words her father had spoken to her on his deathbed: "Ephie, I want you to be strong and courageous."

In the days to come, she would have to draw on those words many times, especially since the year she took on the role of CEO coincided not only with her beloved father's death but also with the 2008 economic downturn.

Yet she had a legion of supporters standing behind her, including her extended family (let's not forget seventy-five foster brothers and sisters) and countless people already familiar with the Ballards and the Neighborhood Christian Center. Ephie had learned that faith moves mountains. She had seen it as a small girl growing up in a frugal household with a kitchen table that always had room for one more. And she had seen it in her father as he was drawing his last breaths.

Ephie remembers it well.

"In his last days, my father showed the ultimate strength. He always taught us to 'know your business.' And that's what he did, up to his very last meal. I watched my father, who could lift a refrigerator by himself and load it into a truck, struggle to lift his fork. But he did. He ate his three meals a day. He was handling his business. He wanted me to go beyond what I thought I could do and where I thought I could go and modeled that for me so many times, right up to the end. Many times I have gone back in my mind to that moment and said, 'Yes! I can be strong and courageous!'"

While Ephie and her parents had known for years that her path was moving parallel to theirs, she shied away from it as a young adult, admiring her parents' work while still wanting to forge her own way.

Gifted with a strong singing voice, she dreamed of becoming a recording artist, but instead, after she earned a bachelor's degree in English, she taught music, music theory, and English in Memphis schools for three years. As she looked at the faces of those children day after day and became heartbroken over their needs, she realized that like her father, she could never be just their teacher.

She knew that she could never sing just for her own gain, teach for her own gain, do *anything* for her own gain.

She had to do something more about all of the needs she saw. It was in her blood.

She married Rodney Johnson, who became her partner in ministry much like Monroe had been for JoeAnn. Ephie and Rodney launched the Neighborhood Christian Center in Decatur, Alabama, and directed it for two years before returning to the NCC in Memphis in 1997. Those years served as a wonderful preparation for the leadership roles they would eventually fill in Memphis.

To initiate the leadership transition, the position of administrative director was created for Ephie; JoeAnn remained executive director and closely mentored Ephie in every aspect of running a ministry. Ephie drove the van, painted the walls, cooked in the kitchen, worked directly with clients, and watched everything her mother did. They worked this way for the next eleven years.

The transition from the elder Ballard's leadership to Ephie as CEO was a subject of interest all over Memphis. Ephie stepped into her mother's shoes slowly, carefully, with the weight of trepidation. She came forward the way noted author and psychoanalyst Clarissa Pinkola Estés once described: when you go toward your destiny, you might go quaking and trembling, but you have to go nevertheless.

"My biggest concern was that I didn't tear up everything in my first year," Ephie says. "That first year, we kept the lights on, nobody was laid off, we didn't lose anything, and from then on we've grown." Like her mother, Ephie is a quick study and has benefited from the counsel of experienced mentors.

Keeping such a large enterprise continually funded and fully staffed is a Herculean task. The need is constant. From the moment the doors opened in the new building, the center has buzzed day and night with activities in the full-court gymnasium, spacious chapel, kitchen, offices, and meeting rooms.

Historically the NCC has enjoyed unusual support from a cadre of faithful private donors. As Ephie puts it, "There are good people in Memphis who write us personal checks for thousands of dollars because they see real grassroots work here."

But the millennium brought a slow downslide in the U.S. economy that took a sudden deep dive in 2008 and created a double whammy for nonprofits like the NCC. "We didn't just lose donors," JoeAnn says, "we gained clients at the same time." Donations slowed down as the numbers of neighbors in need increased.

Just as JoeAnn had to make her way so many years earlier as an African American woman trying to raise funds, Ephie has needed to find her approach as well.

Like her parents, Ephie is generally one of the tallest people in any room. But more than owning sheer physical stature, she possesses a commanding presence that appears effortless. People are drawn to her charismatic personality and listen to what she has to say.

As a member of the next generation of Ballards, she has had the opportunity to garner the attention of the children of aging donors who have been faithfully committed to the work of the senior Ballards. She speaks to civic groups, hosts luncheons that allow busy businesspeople in downtown Memphis to hear the mission of the NCC over their lunch break, and sings and speaks in churches.

While many things differ between her style and her parents', one important thread remains the same.

She prays.

She prays with the same trust her parents had: that the work belongs to God and that God will provide for it.

Under Ephie's leadership, while the food pantry and clothes closet remain strong programs, she and JoeAnn have a shared vision: to reach back earlier into a child's life, and extend help further into adulthood, providing a continuum of support in a person's life.

From the time Gene Cashman first saw the NCC in action while packing Christmas baskets in the center's earliest days, he was drawn to the Ballards' work. When Cashman was tapped to run what eventually became The Urban Child Institute, he and JoeAnn found themselves in constant dialogue.

He has called her "a sage" and brought her onto the Urban Child Institute's board of directors, where she served for nine years, five of those years as the chair. The institute, with its acronym UCI, is a think tank dedicated to the well-being and health of children from in utero to age three in Memphis.

When JoeAnn rotated off the board, UCI kept an office space in their building devoted to her use.

"We were always educating each other," JoeAnn says. "Gene educated me about the upper echelons of Memphis, and I educated him about the poor of Memphis. Through the years we got closer and wound up merging our thoughts and saying, 'Let's work together.'"

A tighter focus on babies and toddlers seemed like a natural next step to JoeAnn, for three reasons. One, decades of compassionate ministry made her a witness to entrenched patterns, life-style choices, and unavoidable conditions of poverty that guarantee a pool of people who cannot give their children the parenting they deserve. "While the poor will always be with us," she said, "they shouldn't be the same poor over and over again." Deliberate measures must be introduced to interrupt generational patterns.

Over the years, JoeAnn also recognized a change in the children she was seeing. Increasingly, they were exposed to violence, both at home and in the community. "When Monroe and I were taking foster children into our home, there was violence, but usually it was a spot thing," she said. "We might have had a parent who was an alcoholic, or we might come across a beating now and then, or a child who was raped by a relative. But someone recognized it and told someone else, and it was dealt with right way. What's different now is both the degree of violence and the level of repetition. These things are happening to the same child over and over again."

Third, at that time, Memphis had the highest infant mortality rate among the nation's sixty largest cities, with babies in Memphis dying at twice the rate of the national average. A 2005 article in the *Commercial Appeal* states, "In 2002, 202 babies didn't see their first birthday—enough to fill 10 kindergarten classrooms. . . .Several Memphis ZIP codes have infant death rates higher than scores of Third World countries. North Memphis's 38108 is deadlier for babies than Vietnam, El Salvador, and Iran. Infant mortality is the barometer of a community's ills: poverty, pollution, crime, lack of education, access to health care, and safe, affordable housing."

Part of the problem was that the word wasn't getting out in Memphis. The article continues, "In the early 1990s cities across the country launched public information campaigns spurred by the federal government to cut infant deaths and bring the United States's rate more in line with other industrialized countries. Memphis never joined up."

This meant that expectant mothers—particularly poor black mothers who were three times more likely to lose their babies than white women for a myriad of reasons—weren't getting even the simplest information that could save their babies' lives, such as the importance of prenatal care and putting babies on their backs to sleep.

The statistics weren't just daunting numbers to JoeAnn. They were the faces of women and babies she had been working with for years.

For Cashman, working with the NCC was a natural next step. He recognized that grassroots, nonprofit organizations are often locked out of the world of academic research that could make their work more effective, while at the same time, academic researchers usually lack regular access to people on the street who could most benefit from their findings.

While UCI was conducting important research on the crucial factors that impact a child's early life but didn't have a way both to translate and convey the information to the people who needed it most. Cashman, along with Hank Herrod—the former Dean of the College of Medicine at the University of Tennessee Center for the Health Sciences and now a Fellow at UCI—felt that the NCC would be a perfect conduit.

"The NCC represents a dissemination mechanism that is unparalleled by anyone in this community," says Cashman. "Through their strong network of pastors, pastors' wives, parishioners, parents, schools, and businesses, we are able to introduce interventions to children all over our city."

JoeAnn and Ephie also believed in the efficacy of the partnership with UCI, and the vision for reaching children at even younger ages started coming to fruition.

Herrod took research on early brain development of babies—showing that a child's brain grows to 80 percent of adult size by the age of three—and prepared reports that he handed over to the NCC. The staff made modifications so that the information would be more accessible to the general public and presented it to local pastors, teachers, and parents.

Their partnership, called Operation Smart Child, supports the NCC in doing what it does best, and the Urban Child Institute has a direct line between the science of early childhood development and impacting the mental, social, economic, and spiritual lives of the children and families who need a safety net. Memphis's infant-mortality rate has dropped by one-third in the last few years, and many attribute the partnership between the NCC and UCI in playing a part in such a dramatic decrease.

In some churches it is common to see Operation Smart Child fliers asking, "Are you pregnant or do you have a child under three years old?"

The fliers invite parents to come to the NCC to learn how to "Touch, Talk, Read, and Play" with their little ones, and in the process they are taught that these simple interactions can stimulate their babies' brains. Expectant parents learn the importance of regular prenatal care and a healthy lifestyle during pregnancy. Parents who regularly attend classes also receive items that help them to better care for their children: baby carriers, booster seats, strollers, diapers, and other baby items.

Seeing how effective churches were at spreading the message of healthy development in young children, Ephie launched First Ladies for Healthy Babies, a network that encourages churches and pastors' wives—the first ladies of the church—to refer neighbors in need who are pregnant or have a child under the age of three. Ephie's goal is that by 2016, they will train five hundred parents to adopt parenting techniques that will raise brain-healthy children.

While the focus on babies has been a major piece of the puzzle for the NCC, perhaps closest to Ephie and Rodney's hearts is the LoveBuilders program, which provides marriage enrichment workshops and activities.

After going through a very difficult season in their own marriage, the Johnsons felt compelled to provide help for the couples in their sphere of influence. There have been some amazing stories of hope and reconciliation born out of the program, led by Rodney. The highlight of the year is the annual marriage retreat—usually in February—when LoveBuilders participants take a bus trip out of town and stay in a hotel for the weekend. These couples have, for the most part, met on a monthly basis all year long and are excited about their group getaway. JoeAnn usually accompanies them.

"JoeAnn called me up early one morning," recalls Hank Herrod, "and said, 'I want you to come over here.' I tried to get her to tell me why, but all she would say is, 'I just want to show you something.'

"It was icy rain, absolutely horrible weather, and there were four or five Greyhound buses filled with couples, headed to Dallas for the LoveBuilders Retreat. She explained to me that most of these couples never had the opportunity or the resources to take a trip together, and many of them had never even been out of Memphis. I had never seen anything like it. These couples wouldn't have cared if there had been a flood; they would've been on those buses!"

One has only to walk the streets of North Memphis on any given day and at any hour and chances are you will run into a person with a story of being helped by the Neighborhood Christian Center.

But because the kind of help they offer is multidimensional, so too is the healing.

If they give an unemployed man a job driving one of their vans, they will also offer him financial tutoring and job training. If they hear of a worthy woman who wants to go to college, folks at the NCC will make phone calls and do their best to find scholarship money. If they help a mother with food and clothing for her baby, they will strive to draw her into their Operation Smart Child program.

More than sixty churches partner with the NCC to reach

out to those in need. The board of directors includes a variety of Christian businesspeople who are committed to using their resources and time to help the poor, and volunteers are still ample and faithful. It has every reason to succeed, but its mission and work are not for the impatient. Like most things that truly matter, believing in the NCC requires foresight as well as farsightedness.

NCC Chairman of the Board Jim Witherington points to the staff's dedication to its clients, "engaging their hearts and empowering them to seek a better life." As evidence of the NCC's effectiveness, he looks at "the expansive network of centers, churches, and affiliates developed by JoeAnn, Monroe, and now Ephie over the last three decades, giving NCC the broadest reach of any Memphis nonprofit. The NCC is a true builder of community, and a key element of our vision for the future is to build up satellite centers to meet the specific needs of each neighborhood. In the process, we are building community—one life at a time."

Ephie stands resolute about the NCC's mission and vision of the future.

"We understand that changing lives takes time," she says. "It takes seven to ten years to help a neighbor in need become independent from a generational, impoverished state of mind. We are committed to staying on the front lines of change, to help create a new generation of people who are ready for work, ready to raise a family, and ready to help their communities. And we are here for the long haul."

Ephie looks back at what she has learned from her parents, just as JoeAnn looked back to her own childhood to recreate community in Memphis. Even as things change, Ephie remembers something that her grandfather—JoeAnn's beloved Montee—would chant to his children to help them focus on what matters instead of chasing after this and that: *Don't run behind pretty things.*

Ephie expresses it in her own words. "We follow God, not needs. There will always be needs, but God asks us to meet some, not all, of them. The goal is not to meet every need, to create a new program every time there is a new need, to have the biggest outreach. The goal is to be faithful to follow the path He has for us, to live the story He is writing for each of us and to let Him weave it with the stories of those around us as He sees fit."

JoeAnn's entire life has been a practice in staying focused on prayerful intention and prayerful deeds. "We do what God says, no matter what it costs or how strange it looks. If we go with the flow of society, people will be marginalized, so we must go against the grain."

She compares a life of service to a tapestry.

"If you look at it from the back, all the threads are tangled, the colors are muted, and the patterns are unclear. But when you turn it over the right way, you see the vibrant colors, the smooth texture, the whole picture. In everyday life, we're usually looking at the underside of our lives. My life has often looked messy and chaotic, though I've occasionally caught a glimpse of what God is weaving together. But I trust that when I serve Him, not only is He making something beautiful of my life but that He is also making something beautiful out of the lives of those I'm serving."

Epilogue

O N A CRISP OCTOBER DAY, JOEANN DRIVES HER van with the window down, carrying a carload of her children and grandchildren to Lucedale. "It feels like camp-meeting weather," she says with a smile.

It's been nearly fifty years since JoeAnn first left the comforts of her childhood home to begin her adventures in Memphis, but she still goes back to the Basin community most years for camp meeting. "When I moved to Memphis, I couldn't put into words what was missing," says JoeAnn. "I missed the shared peas and okra, the homemade clothes, the adults talking quietly on the porch after a long day while the kids played in the backyard. It wasn't that I was romanticizing the 'good ole days.'" Instead, she explains, that based on her reality of growing up in a community of giving and receiving, she had a desire to recreate that spirit of unity whenever she saw broken relationships.

Recreating community is exactly what the Ballard family has been doing in Memphis all these years. JoeAnn calls what God has built through them "a network of compassion," an idea based on what she saw modeled for her.

"In Basin, if someone needed a doctor and there wasn't time to drive to the next city to get the doctor," she remembers, "there was always someone we could call who knew enough about medicine to help. If someone needed to go to the store but didn't have a car, there was always a person with a car in the community who would either drive you or pick up what you needed. It wasn't talked about; it was just *done*. I get so sad when I hear how many family members so easily put loved ones in the hospital or a nursing home. We've become a 'let somebody else do it' society."

JoeAnn believes that this mentality of shirking responsibilities comes from living in a busy society. "The funny things is that most of us are busy doing nothing and don't even realize it," she says. "We are going places we don't want to go with people we don't like. Most people eventually come to the realization that was really mattered was relationships. All of the other things will fade eventually. Clothes either go out of style or no longer fit, cars stop working, and houses get leaks. Relationships, on the other hand, continue to change and grow. Possessions suck away our resources and energy while relationships give life."

JoeAnn recalls a camp meeting long ago, when she and Monroe had been working with the NCC for fifteen years. A secret party had been planned to celebrate the work they were doing in Memphis. "Rather than celebrating my husband and me," she says, "the celebration was really about what the Basin community had produced. People don't leave Basin to get a better job; instead, they leave Basin to reproduce what has been produced in them. I could pick almost any person who has left and could show you that he or she is still a servant."

This same spirit of servanthood has passed into each of the Ballard children.

In the same way that Ephie could not deny the call to serve, neither could her siblings. Linda runs the NCC's Baby and Me program—part of Operation Smart Child—and her husband, Carlos Williams, directs youth and college programs. Monroe Jr. married Janice, one of the last three girls Monroe and JoeAnn took in, and the two of them now raise foster children. Monroe Jr. owns his own video production company and volunteers his skills for NCC projects. Justin has a mind for business and a love for music and volunteers his musical talents for NCC functions. Many of the Ballards' foster children work or volunteer for the NCC in some capacity, including serving as missionaries in their own neighborhoods.

JoeAnn and her children walk around the hallowed grounds at camp meeting again, with a tightening in their throats as they remember so many loved ones who once walked those grounds never to walk there again. On Sunday morning when it's time for the Love Feast, JoeAnn looks into the eyes of her children as she passes bread to them.

The age-old words come alive in her deep-throated voice: "God has done this for me, and He has done this for you."

And there is enough bread for everyone.

Partial List of Sources

Ballard, Monroe, and JoeAnn Ballard. Serving in the City: Nurturing the Poor to Independence (Kansas City: Beacon Hill Press, 1986).

Ballard, JoeAnn, with Susan Autry Currier. I Belong Here: A Biography of Community (Fulton, KY: The Master Design, 2005).

Barrett, Katherine, Monroe Ballard, and JoeAnn Ballard. Room in Our Hearts, Room in Our Home (Nashville: Impact Books / The Benson Company, 1979).

Edmondson, Aimee. "Infant Mortality in Memphis," The Commercial Appeal, March 6, 2005.

Evans, Rachel Held, "Bootstraps and Safety Nets: Some thoughts on generational poverty in America." Accessed February 10, 2014, http://rachelheldevans.com/blog/bootstraps-and-safety-nets-some-thoughts-on-generational-poverty-in-america.

Fowler, Cary. "The Progressive Farmer: A Long Row's Hoeing into Lespedeza," published in Southern Changes: The Journal of the Southern Regional Council (1978-2003), Vol. 1, No. 10, 1979, pp. 4, 29-32. Accessed October 3, 2012 from Beck Library, Emory University online, http://beck.library.emory.edu/southernchanges/article.php?id=sc01-10_003.

Myers, Bryant L. Walking with the Poor: Principles and Practices of Transformational Development (Maryknoll, NY: Orbis Books, 1999).

Nees, Thomas G. Compassion Evangelism: Meeting Human Needs (Kansas City: Beacon Hill Press, 1996).

General background information from the Tennessee Historical Society. The Tennessee Encyclopedia of History and Culture. Last modified 2014, http://tennesseeencyclopedia.net.

Statistics

Cozzens, Lisa. The Civil Rights Movement 1955–1965. African American History. Accessed March, 2014, http://www.watson.org/~lisa/blackhistory/civilrights-55-65/missippi.html.

1960 Census of Population and Housing. Accessed April 15, 2014, http://www.census.gov/prod/www/abs/decennial/1960.html.

2011 HHS Poverty Guidelines. Accessed April 15, 2014, http://aspe.hhs.gov/poverty/11poverty.shtml.

Memphis History

Waller, Marguerite, and Jennifer Rycenga, eds. Frontline Feminisms: Women, War, and Resistance (New York: Routledge, 2001), p. 382.

Yellow Fever: The Plague of Memphis. Accessed April 15, 2014, http://historic-memphis.com/memphis/yellow-fever/yellow-fever.html.

"Negroes in Tennessee" from Tennessee: A Guide to the State. Accessed December 12, 2012, http://newdeal.feri.org/guides/tnguide/ch10.htm.

Hamilton, Green Polonius. The Bright Side of Memphis: a Compendium of Information Concerning the Colored People of Memphis, Tennessee. (Memphis: G. P. Hamilton, 1908). Accessed December 2012, http://onlinebooks.library.upenn.edu/webbin/book/lookupname?key=Hamilton%2c%20Green%20Polonius%2c%201867.

Chickasaw

Hodge, Frederick Webb, compiler. The Handbook of American Indians North of Mexico. Bureau of American Ethnology, Government Printing Office (Washington: 1906). Access Genealogy. Last updated January 29, 2012, http://www.accessgenealogy.com/native/chickasaw-tribe.htm.

Chucalissa

"Chucalissa." University of Memphis, C. H. Nash Museum. Last updated February 24, 2014, http://www.memphis.edu/chucalissa/about.htm.

Civil War in Memphis

ORA—War of the Rebellion; a compilation of the official records of the Union and Confederate Armies, 70 volumes in four series; Washington: US Government Printing Office, 1880—1901. ORN—Official records of the Union and Confederate Navies in the War of the Rebellion, 30 volumes in two series; Washington: US Government Printing Office, 1894—1922. Wikipedia. Last updated March 14, 2014, http://en.wikipedia.org/wiki/Battle_of_Memphis#cite_note-9.

Martin Luther King Jr. 1999 Assassination Trial

"Complete Transcript of the Martin Luther King Jr. Assassination Conspiracy Trial." Ratical.org. Published online December 8, 1999, http://ratical.org/ratville/JFK/MLKACT/MLKACT-vol14.html#VERDICT.

Martin Luther King, Jr. Nobel Prize

Nobelprize.org. Nobel Media AB 2013. Accessed April 13, 2014, http://www.nobelprize.org/nobel_prizes/peace/laureates/1964/king-bio.html.

Memphis and Charleston Railroad

"Memphis and Charleston Railroad," Wikipedia. Last updated April 8, 2014, http://en.wikipedia.org/wiki/Memphis_and_Charleston_Railroad.

Mississippi River

Ash, Stephen V. Middle Tennessee Society Transformed, 1860–1870: War and Peace in the Upper South (Knoxville: University of Tennessee Press, 1988).

Burman, Ben L., and Alice Caddy. Look Down That Winding River: An Informal Portrait of the Mississippi (New York: Taplinger, 1973).

Gateway! New Orleans, "The Mississippi River." Accessed December 13, 2012, http://www.gatewayno.com/history/Mississippi.html.

Morris, Wright, ed. The Mississippi River Reader (New York: Doubleday Anchor, 1962).

Twain, Mark, Life on the Mississippi (Boston: James R. Osgood and Company, 1883; reprinted 1957).

Seymour, Digby G. Divided Loyalties: Fort Sanders and the Civil War in East Tennessee (Knoxville: East Tennessee Historical Society, 1982).

People

"Martin Luther King Jr. Acceptance Speech." Nobelprize.org. Nobel Media AB 2013.Accessed February 22, 2013, http://www.nobelprize.org/mediaplayer/index.php?id=1853.

Poverty

Evans, Rachel Held. Bootstraps and Safety Nets: Some Thoughts on Generational Poverty in America, quoting Amanda Opelt. Accessed April 15, 2014, http://rachelheldevans.com/blog/bootstraps-and-safety-nets-some-thoughts-on-generational-poverty-in-america.

Religion

Brother Lawrence: "The Practice of the Presence of God: The Best Rule of Holy Life," Christian Classics Ethereal Library. Accessed December 24, 2012, http://www.ccel.org/ccel/lawrence/practice.pdf.

Audio Files

Nash, Ken, and Mimi Rosenberg. "Building Bridges: Dr. King: Memphis City Sanitation Workers Strike," interview with sanitation workers re: 1968 strike and Martin Luther King Jr. Internet Archive. Accessed December 31, 2012, http://archive. org/search.php?query=memphis%201960%20audio.

15601550R00089

Made in the USA
San Bernardino, CA
01 October 2014